The CaReeR CoWaRd's Guide™ to
Job Searching

**Sensible Strategies
for Overcoming
Job Search Fears**

Katy Piotrowski, M.Ed.

The Career Coward's Guide to Job Searching

© 2009 by Katy Piotrowski

7321 Shadeland Station, Suite 200
Indianapolis, IN 46256-3923
Phone: 800-648-JIST   Fax: 877-454-7839   E-mail: info@jist.com

Visit our Web site at **www.jist.com** for information on JIST, free job search tips, tables of contents and sample pages, and ordering instructions for our many products!

See the back of this book for additional JIST titles and ordering information. Quantity discounts are available for JIST books. Have future editions of JIST books automatically delivered to you on publication through our convenient standing order program. Please call our Sales Department at 800-648-5478 for a free catalog and more information.

Trade Product Manager: Lori Cates Hand
Development Editor: Aaron Black
Cover Designer: Alan Evans
Illustrator: Chris Sabatino
Interior Designer: Amy Adams
Page Layout: Toi Davis
Proofreaders: Paula Lowell, Jeanne Clark
Indexer: Cheryl Lenser

Printed in the United States of America
13 12 11 10 09 08 9 8 7 6 5 4 3 2 1

Library of Congress Cataloging-in-Publication Data

Piotrowski, Katy, 1962-

The career coward's guide to job searching : sensible strategies for overcoming job search fears / by Katy Piotrowski.

p. cm.

Includes index.
ISBN 978-1-59357-392-8 (alk. paper)
1. Job hunting. I. Title.
HF5382.7.P565 2008
650.14--dc22

2008021159

We have been careful to provide accurate information in this book, but it is possible that errors and omissions have been introduced. Please consider this in making any career plans or other important decisions. Trust your own judgment above all else and in all things.

Trademarks: All brand names and product names used in this book are trade names, service marks, trademarks, or registered trademarks of their respective owners.

ISBN 978-1-59357-392-8

About This Book

Job searching is tough. It can feel as if you're peddling yourself like a common product to get the attention of employers. "Why can't a great company just *know* that I'd be an asset and make me an offer? Why do I have to play this stupid game?" you might think. Add to this the confusion of sorting through a rat's nest of job search activities: online job sites, classified advertisements, recruiters, networking…and on and on. Arggh! Where in the world do you begin, and which avenues are best?

I agree with you: Job searching is tough. Yet being unemployed or in a poor-fit job is even tougher—especially when you have excellent skills and experience to offer, and you just want to find an opportunity to use them.

But what if you had a proven, effective, step-by-step process to follow? What if you knew what to do first, second, and so on, to achieve the job search results you want? Would you feel a little more positive about pushing forward?

If your answer is yes, I'm so glad we found each other! In your hands is a gem of a book that will show you *exactly* how to job search to find the positions you want. *The Career Coward's Guide to Job Searching* shows you which activities make the most sense for your situation, and how to execute them effectively through doable steps that lead to big results.

Sound good? Then take a peek inside right now and check out the "Risk It or Run From It" boxes at the start of each chapter. Notice how in just a few seconds, you can find out what the recommended activity is all about, how long it will take for you to complete it, and what else you can do if you want to skip it altogether. You're in control!

When you do decide to invest your time and effort in a recommended activity, you can be confident that the techniques *work*. Not only have they been shown to be effective by some of the leading job search and research experts in the country, I've been using them successfully, day after day, with thousands of my own career counseling clients.

And here's the best part: You'll learn how to land your next great job, *plus* gain the know-how to cultivate the next job search after that, and throughout the rest of your career. Better and better career opportunities will keep coming your way. You don't need to be afraid of job searching anymore.

I'm excited to have this success happen for you. Let's get started!

—Kathy P.

Dedication

*To Mark Granovetter, who showed me how
to make sense out of job search chaos.*

Contents

Acknowledgements

This is the fifth book in the *Career Coward's* series. It's been a huge amount of work for me, as well as for my family and friends. I owe so much gratitude to Pete, Ada, and J.P., for supporting me as I've holed up in my writing corner weekend after weekend to meet my deadlines. Thanks also go to my friends (especially the Soup Supper crowd!) for waiting patiently for my time to be more open once again.

Thanks also to my clients and colleagues, who provide the inspiration and input for these books. Every day, you inspire me to discover and communicate better ways to envision and achieve career nirvana. I learn so much from you!

Finally, to my editors Lori Cates Hand and Aaron Black, and my book promotion team Natalie Ostrom, Selena Dehne, and Carrie Pinsky, thank you for believing in and supporting me, day after day, week after week. You've made my foray into the publishing world a wonderful, memorable experience of a lifetime.

Turn Your Job Search Fears into Fantastic Results

Y ou're job searching. You're motivated to find a position just right for you—one that makes great use of your unique talents and skills, and rewards you well. It's about time that you landed in a better job!

Yet you're probably a little scared, too. Will anyone even want what you have to offer? And with so many ways to job search—Web sites, networking groups, having your resume distributed far and wide—how will you decide which plan will lead to the best results? It can be overwhelming!

But take a deep breath, exhale, and know that right now, in your hands, you hold an excellent guide and cheerleader to help you succeed. This little book will take the guesswork out of how to conduct a successful job search, *plus* provide you helpful encouragement through each doable step along the way. Hey, chances are pretty good that you might even have *fun*! And when you finish reading the last page and close the book, you will have accomplished something very, very valuable: You will now know how to locate and land positions that are a great match for what you have to offer—a skill that will serve you well throughout your career.

Sound good? Want to learn more? Okay, read on...

How to Use This Book to Achieve Your Job Search Goals

The Career Cowards Guide to Job Searching will walk you through a proven, step-by-step process for overcoming your fears and landing the positions you want. Each chapter in *The Career Cowards Guide to Job Searching* will provide you with techniques that have been tried, tested, and perfected on thousands of other Career Cowards. And to make this valuable information even more fun and easy to use, each chapter includes an at-a-glance "Risk It or Run From It" status box, providing you the following vital information:

- **Risk Rating:** From "No risk at all" to "This is a deal breaker!" you'll quickly see how harmless or hazardous each step will be.

- **Payoff Potential:** Find out what's in it for you if you do decide to take the risk and complete the step. The payoff might be enough to push you through any fear holding you back.

- **Time to Complete:** Whether it's a few minutes, a few hours, or longer, you'll know in advance how much time each activity will take.

- **Bailout Strategy:** Absolutely refuse to put in the time or take the risk for a particular step? You have other options; find out what they are.

- **The "20 Percent Extra" Edge:** Learn how braving the recommended steps will give you a significant advantage over your competition.

- **"Go For It!" Bonus Activity:** Feeling really courageous? Push your success even further with this suggested activity.

Each information-packed chapter also includes

- A "how-to" section, providing clear, motivating instructions for each activity.

- Information about "Why It's Worth Doing," helping you to understand the purpose behind each interviewing recommendation.

- "Panic Point!" highlights, pointing out and troubleshooting areas Career Cowards find especially challenging.

- An encouraging "Career Champ Profile," describing a real-life example of a Career Coward who succeeded after conquering a challenging job search fear.

- The "Core Courage Concept," boiling down the chapter's key points into an inspiring message.

- And a "Confidence Checklist," providing you an at-a-glance review of the chapter's primary action items.

As you move through the chapters of this book, you'll learn how to implement and succeed with the following proven job search action plan:

- We'll begin by discussing which job hunting methods truly produce the best results. The data I provide come from reliable, credible sources, so you can feel confident about building your plan around my recommendations.

- You'll then assess your current job search strategy against what has been shown to work most successfully to quickly identify opportunities to significantly improve your results.

- From there, I'll help you determine your ideal job search focus, as well as show you how to find hundreds of companies that might be interested in adding you to their teams.

- Once you've established your successful job search foundation, we'll dive into the nuts and bolts of the process—developing your resume and cover letter, and learning effective strategies for responding to posted positions.

- We'll also discuss, in depth, how to find and tap into the 70 percent or more of positions that never get advertised.

These strategies will boost your confidence, land you better jobs, and change your life!

- Moving into the home stretch, I'll show you how to pull together all of this valuable information into a doable, highly successful plan that you can implement day-to-day to achieve the results you want.

- You'll also learn how to respond to the interviews and opportunities that will soon be coming your way, so that you ultimately land a motivating, rewarding position.

- And to help ensure your future successes, I'll show you how to keep building on your momentum to achieve even greater career achievements after you've landed your next job.

This is an energizing, enlightening process that I'm excited to share with you. But before we jump in, read about how one job searcher implemented the strategies in this book with an excellent payoff.

Career Champ Profile: Daniel

After the tragedy of 9/11, Daniel found himself among the hundreds of thousands of unemployed workers who had been laid off, desperately seeking work, but finding few opportunities. After six months of job searching, Daniel decided to set aside his career as a mechanical engineer, and instead work with his wife supporting her accounting business. Although he longed to be a part of the challenging technology development projects he'd worked on earlier in his career, his discouragement over his job search results kept him from trying again.

Three years later, still greatly missing the challenges and rewards of his former engineering career, Daniel contacted me wondering whether I'd be able to help him conduct a more successful job search. "I'm pretty skeptical that there will be anything out there for me—especially since I've been out of the industry for four years now, and now I'm in my 50s—but I at least want to give it a try."

Daniel and I started his job search process by first determining the type of work he was aiming for (project management at an engineering technology company), as well as a long list of potential employers. As we researched and built a target list of possible companies, Daniel's confidence began rising. "There are many more businesses out there than I realized!" he said excitedly, as we reviewed databases and directories together.

Once we were clear on the type of position Daniel wanted, as well as the companies that might be a good fit for him, we were then able to develop targeted job search documents for him—a resume, cover letters, portfolio, thank-you notes, and so on—customized to his career goals. Within just a few days, Daniel had his plan and tools pulled together and was raring to go.

He began his search by connecting with people he knew from earlier positions he'd held, as well as with some contacts I was able to provide. He talked with these contacts both in person at coffee shops, as well as over the phone. In these conversations, he learned a little about his contacts' personal and professional lives, discussed his job search goals while sharing details about his background and accomplishments, and brainstormed next steps that would move him toward his goals. These conversations turned out to be highly motivating and productive for Daniel, and within a month, he'd spoken with more than 20 people, including a number of hiring managers at his target companies.

In addition to the people connections he was making, Daniel also presented himself to several of the potential employers on his target list—even though most of them had no openings advertised. Daniel let them know he was interested in their companies and was available as a resource. This activity began producing interviews quickly. Daniel also continued to keep an eye on, and respond to, posted job advertisements that were a good fit for his background.

Within just eight weeks, Daniel had launched and was executing a highly successful job search. He was busy every day connecting with potential employers and getting closer and closer to realizing his dream of landing another challenging, rewarding position in the technology industry. And all of his hard work eventually paid off: Less than three months after relaunching his search, Daniel accepted an offer for a position paying 20 percent more than he'd hoped to earn. But even better than the impressive job he landed, Daniel had learned how to overcome his fear of job searching. "I won't be afraid of the process next time," Daniel told me. "I have great things to offer, and now I know how to connect successfully with potential employers. I feel great about what I've accomplished, as well as my future career path. I'm excited and motivated again!"

Part 1

Understand What Successful Job Searching Looks Like

Chapter 1

Discover What Really Works

You want a job—not just any job, but a *great* one. And you want to find it as quickly and as painlessly as possible. You've tried your own methods of job searching, but seeing as you're reading this book, you're probably not very happy with the results. You're ready to learn better ways to achieve your career and job search goals.

If this sounds like you, you've chosen the right resource to help you improve your job hunting results, now and in the future. In this chapter, and on through to the final page, I'll introduce you to job search activities that get the best results, plus show you step-by-step strategies for executing them easily and successfully. I'll start by giving you a little information on what the researchers say works best in job search, and then share my own experiences, based on observing the results of thousands of job hunters. We have a lot of ground to cover, so let's get started!

Risk It or Run From It?

- **Risk Rating:** Low. You're just learning a few basics to set you up for success.

(continued)

(continued)

- **Payoff Potential:** Huge! Learning from the successes and failures of others can save you lots of wasted time and effort.

- **Time to Complete:** About five minutes (the time it will take you to read this chapter).

- **Bailout Strategy:** If you don't need data to convince you to adopt the job search strategies I recommend, skip on to Chapter 2.

- **The "20 Percent Extra" Edge:** Rather than operating on a "What I've always done" approach, you'll be benefiting from a "What works best" plan.

- **"Go For It!" Bonus Activity:** Conduct a Google search of effective job search studies to learn more about what works well.

How to Shift Your Job Search from Failure to Success!

Ready to learn which activities will produce better results in your job search? Read on to find out more about what studies of job searching reveal, as well as the real-life results of thousands of job searchers.

Consider the Data Behind What Works

Years ago, when I began my first job as a career counselor right after graduate school, I kept hearing over and over about the "hidden job market." "The best jobs are often not even advertised," my more experienced colleagues would say. But the small voice in my head would wonder, "How do you *know* the best jobs aren't advertised? On what data are you basing this statement?"

After a few months of hearing this daily declaration, I decided to seek out the source (if there was one!) of this hidden market statement. After searching around for a while, I found, in small type on one of the documents my employer used to educate our clients about effective job searching methods, a citation referencing a book called, *Getting a Job: A Study of Contacts and Careers*, by Mark Granovetter, published in 1974. I tracked it down, and slogged through the pages and pages of statistical information.

The book reports on several studies about how individuals find jobs, in particular, describing the results of two studies conducted through Harvard University. Finding after finding in this book showed that in the majority of cases—80 percent or more—job searchers located and landed jobs through nonadvertised avenues. Rather than reading and responding to ads, the job hunters they studied had faster results, and found better jobs, through personal contacts and applying directly to companies.

"Ah ha!" I thought. "This is the 'hidden job market' people describe!" and I concluded that the word "hidden" was being used because the opportunities those job searchers uncovered weren't obvious to the world as a whole. "Okay," I said to myself, "So here's some concrete data to back up the hidden market claims I've been hearing."

Since uncovering that study data years ago, I've kept tabs on other, more current studies, describing how job hunters locate and land jobs. The data continues to show that jobs come through the three primary avenues Granovetter described in *Getting a Job*: posted ads, personal contacts, and approaching companies directly. From study to study, the actual percentages of jobs found in each of these categories shifts slightly, between 20 to 30 percent of individuals finding jobs through ads, and 30 percent or more finding positions through connections and direct approach methods. Over time, I rounded the figures into these rough approximations:

- One-third of jobs are found through job ads

- One-third of jobs are found through personal connections

- One-third of jobs are found through approaching companies directly

This made describing effective job hunting methods and planning job search activities for the clients I was supporting clearer and easier.

Factor in the Results of Real-World Job Searchers

Now that I had some actual data about how job seekers find jobs, I decided to compare the research to what my clients were actually experiencing in their job searches. Yet as soon as I started my "real world" evaluation, I discovered something a little bit shocking: The vast majority of the job hunters I talked to (90 percent or more) *were using job ads as their primary—and often only—activity in job searching.* After a few months of hearing, "I'm mostly looking at job postings, online and in the newspaper," over and over, month after month, from job hunters who were extremely frustrated with their results, I realized that most job hunters were simply missing out on the best job opportunities available!

This was a sad, yet somewhat exciting, realization. "If the majority of job searchers only look into job ads," I thought to myself, "then there's a *huge* opportunity to help my clients significantly improve their job search results by using more effective avenues!"

Since crystallizing this realization, I've made it my mission to help my clients achieve fast, fabulous job search results based on what job search research shows to be most effective, and the clients who have followed this strategy have achieved excellent results.

Why It's Worth Doing

In your life, you've most likely heard someone say, "Why should I change? I've *always* done it this way." And that's fine...as long as what that person does is working! But for many people (and if you're reading this book, you're most likely one of them), the job search methods they've *always* used just aren't getting them the results they want. If this describes you, you're faced with a choice: Do you keep doing the same things, over and over, hoping for a different result...or do you try some new approaches?

It can be easier to convince yourself to try something new if you base your decisions on quality research data, rather than opinions. When it comes to finding a job—a major source of your income, meaning, and satisfaction in life—it makes sense to follow the approaches that the experts say are most effective.

Career Champ Profile: Mason

Mason, a client, is strongly influenced by research. With a master's degree in economics, he challenged my statements that the majority of the jobs—and the best ones, at that—would not be found in online job ads or the newspapers. "For the best results, you'll want to spend most of your time approaching companies directly, and connecting with individuals who can assist your job search, rather than just finding and applying to job ads," I said.

"I don't get it," he countered. "Why wouldn't an employer just run a job posting if he had a need for someone new? In my opinion, that would be the most efficient way to find a new employee." I then spent some time explaining to Mason that hiring managers are busy, and that sorting through a pile of 100 or more applicants hoping to find a few good candidates is much less appealing than hiring a candidate that someone they trust has recommended. Also, I explained that a resume submitted in response to a job ad is much less compelling than being contacted by a candidate who has researched and is interested in your company.

Finally I said to Mason, "Here, borrow this book, *Getting a Job*, by Mark Granovetter. Look at the data and then make a decision for yourself."

Two months later, Mason accepted a very attractive offer for a job he'd learned about through a contact he made on LinkedIn. "In the end, it turned out that reports in *Getting a Job*, and what you were suggesting that I do in my job search, were right. I uncovered better jobs through contacts, and by approaching my target companies directly."

Core Courage Concept

Frustrated with the results of your job search efforts—but scared to attempt some of the activities described so far, such as connecting with people or approaching companies directly? It can feel like you're stuck between a rock and a hard place! It takes guts to say, "What I'm doing isn't working so well. Even though it feels a little scary, I need to try something new." And when it comes to your livelihood, you want to minimize the time you waste, and the opportunities you miss, as quickly as possible.

> ### Confidence Checklist
>
> ☐ Consider the data behind what works.
>
> ☐ Factor in the results of real-world job searches.

Chapter 2

Analyze Your Own Job Search History

Y ou've chugged along, pouring your time and effort into your job search, but gotten dismal results. You've wondered, "What am I doing wrong?" Or, even worse, "What's wrong with me?" Well, this chapter will help you pinpoint your current job search weaknesses, as well as identify specific ways to boost your job search results through more effective strategies.

Risk It or Run From It?

- **Risk Rating:** It might hurt your ego a little to take a hard look at your current job search strategy, but bottom line, the risk in this step is very low.

- **Payoff Potential:** Outstanding! Do you know how good it feels to finally find out how to stop doing things that are ineffective? Here's your chance!

- **Time to Complete:** About 15–30 minutes.

- **Bailout Strategy:** If you already know that your job search strategy would benefit from a major overhaul, and you don't

(continued)

(continued)

> need to know the nitty-gritty details of what you need to improve, move on to chapter 3.
>
> - **The "20 Percent Extra" Edge:** Analyzing your job search activities as compared to the results you're getting—a step very few job searchers ever take—can quickly show you where you can improve your strategy to move ahead faster in your career.
>
> - **"Go For It!" Bonus Activity:** In addition to analyzing your activities for this job search campaign, scrutinize your activities and results for former job hunts you've conducted. This will provide an even better picture of your patterns and opportunities.

How to Analyze Your Current Job Search Approach and Identify Improvements

A few years ago, I met with Sherry, a CPA, to have her take a look at how I was handling my bookkeeping for my career counseling practice. After eight years in business, I knew it was time to get an expert's opinion. Even though meeting with Sherry felt like the "right" thing to do, I was still dreading it. I pictured Sherry shaking her finger at me and berating me for the choices I'd made—but it didn't turn out that way at all.

For the first 15 minutes, Sherry methodically looked through my different accounts and records; then she turned to me and said, "You've got great information to work with here. We're going to set up your books a little differently for next year, but we don't need to change everything you're doing. We'll just make some tweaks." Sherry then created a new bookkeeping file for my business, with slightly different accounts, and walked me through how I should be using the new process.

Over the next few weeks, I worked with her system, even though it felt a little odd at first. And after a few months, I had a wonderful revelation: I was spending less time on bookkeeping (a task I really don't enjoy very much), yet I felt much *better* about my results. I also liked that Sherry, an expert, had recommended a sound plan to me that I could follow. I could clearly see that her process was better. An analysis I'd dreaded at the beginning led to an outstanding result!

That's my goal in helping you analyze your current job search activities—working with you to look at what you've been doing, and to identify opportunities for improvements. Let's get started!

Make Notes About Your Current Job Search Process

For this step, I need you to analyze how you've been job searching to this point. Some job searchers keep records of their activities, either in a notebook, or in a collection of papers. If you have any records like these, gather up those materials. Other job searchers don't keep records at all, and that's okay, too. If not keeping records is more your style, I'm going to ask you to guess your best about what you've been doing.

Either using the records you've gathered, or by recalling your activities, answer these questions:

- "What job search activities have I been using?" For instance, you might have been keeping your eye on job ads posted in the newspaper, on company or employment service Web pages, or on Internet job search sites. These are the most common activities for most job searchers. You might also have been researching potential employers and presenting yourself to them directly, even though no job openings are advertised. Or you might be connecting with colleagues, friends, and support groups to learn about opportunities.

  As you review your job search activities to this point, do your best to divide them into three categories:

- Responding to job ads, such as those posted on Internet job sites, in the newspaper, or on company or employment service Web sites.

- Approaching potential employers directly, even though no job ad is advertised.

- Connecting with colleagues and groups to learn about opportunities in the market.

- "How much time have I been spending on each of these activities each week?" Make a "best guess" estimate of how much time you're putting into applying to ads, presenting yourself directly to potential employers, and connecting with others. Be *honest* with yourself. No one is looking over your shoulder judging your situation. Our goal (yours and mine) is to get an accurate picture of what you've been doing, so that we can figure out how to make improvements that will get you the job search results you want. Here are a few guidelines for determining how much time you're spending on each of these activities:

  - Estimate how much time it takes you to search for and locate job ads to respond to, customize a resume and/or cover letter for each job ad, fill out an online or hardcopy application form, and submit and follow up on your materials. Based on the experiences of the job searchers I've worked with, a single application can take from between five minutes to five hours, so estimate what seems typical for you. Once you've determined the "per application" timeframe, multiply it by the average number of applications you respond to each week.

  - Determine how much time you devote to researching potential employers each week, and to approaching them directly. This might involve surfing the Internet to learn about companies, customizing a cover letter and/ or resume, and then either mailing your materials or stopping by the company to drop them off. This activity might also include the time you put into following up on the materials you've submitted. Again, estimate your average "per company" timeframe, and multiply it by the number of direct approach attempts you complete each week.

- Approximate how much time you spend connecting with people, including colleagues, friends, and groups, to uncover information about potential needs in the job market. Be sure to factor in the time you spend setting up connection opportunities, talking with contacts, and following up on any opportunities you discover. Calculate the total time you devote to these connections weekly.

Compare Your Activities to the "Ideal" Job Search Model

Now that you have a pretty good idea about how you're spending you job search time each week, create a pie picture of your activities, using the following circle:

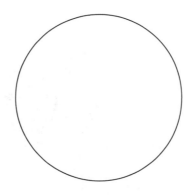

Based on my experience with job searchers, often their job search activities pie will look like this:

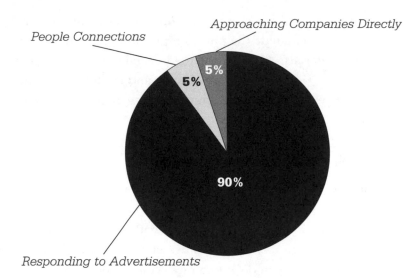

Identify Some Potential Areas for Improvement

This next step isn't rocket science. Evaluate your pie chart against this "ideal" pie chart of job search activities:

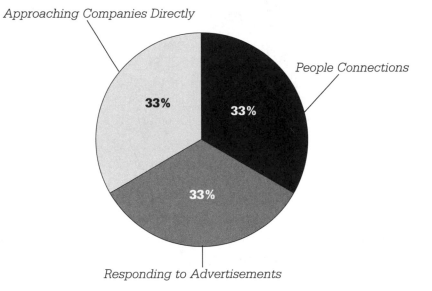

How did the two charts stack up? If you're like most job searchers, you probably discovered that the majority of your time and effort in job searching are spent in responding to ads, and that approaching companies directly and connecting with people are pretty small in comparison. If this is the case, you can take comfort in knowing that there are some *very* simple changes you can make to your job search strategy that will produce much better results for you. We'll cover these activities—and how to execute them—in the next several chapters. And before you know it, your pie chart (and your job search results) will improve significantly.

Panic Point! Are you thinking, "Oh, no! Is the rest of this book going to be about how I need to push myself on potential employers, or connect with strangers, like some obnoxious, desperate job hunter? If so, I'm done with this book *now.*" Before you slam this book closed, hear me out: I can't *force* you to do anything. My hope is that you'll read about and consider the information here (these are job search strategies that *truly* work) before you make any final decisions. If, after you've reviewed the strategies I present, you decide it's not for you, you can feel good knowing that you've at least considered *all* of the information. Have you ever changed your mind about a subject after you've gathered more information? Well, that might happen for you here, so hang in there with me!

Why It's Worth Doing

Day after day in my career counseling practice, I talk to qualified, motivated, career-minded job searchers experiencing high levels of frustration because their job searches aren't going well. These are men and women who are typically confident, happy people, but are pouring out their hearts to me (often reaching for the tissue box!) over the pain they're experiencing. "I have so much to offer," they plead with me. "Why can't I land a good job? What's wrong with me?"

On the other side of the table, I regularly participate in business planning forums attended by company owners and executives. What I hear from them is, "Why can't I find the right people to fill the key positions inside my company? We have so much to offer to the right people. Where are they?"

In my spot between the job searchers and the hiring managers, it's become obvious to me that this dilemma is definitely not a problem of adequate resources; there are plenty of qualified workers and an abundance of challenging positions. Rather, the issue is a communication problem—the two sides just aren't connecting! And it's gotten to the point where it almost seems like a tragic comedy: Both sides are running around in circles wringing their hands in frustration, yet the answers to their problems reside with each other.

My hope for you in reading and considering the ideas in this book is that you'll look at your job search as more of a challenge in communicating the right information to the right people, rather than being forced to do things you really don't want to do. The world needs your talent and expertise, so let's do our best to let them know what you have to offer!

Career Champ Profile: Maureen

Maureen had achieved hundreds of impressive accomplishments in her 15-year career with a Fortune 100 company. She'd received numerous awards, consistently surpassed the goals set for her in her role as store manager, and completed an MBA to build her knowledge and expertise. When an internal company conflict motivated her to resign, Maureen found herself hunting for a job for the first time in many years.

She did what most job searchers do when they find themselves looking for work: Each day, she would wake up, grab a cup of coffee, and shuffle over to her computer to log on to Web sites advertising jobs. "I can do this job...and this one...and this one..." she'd think to herself, reading through the ads. She'd then write up cover letter after cover letter, and customize her resume for each opportunity, before submitting her applications. After a month of this activity, however, Maureen started to get frustrated. She'd heard back from only a few of the companies she'd applied to, and landed only one job interview…for a job she really wasn't excited about at all.

"I'm a smart, capable person," Maureen thought to herself many times. "Why aren't these companies interested in me?" After two months of this exasperating activity, Maureen came to talk to me. "Is there something wrong with me?" she asked, tears filling her eyes. I spent a few minutes asking her about what she'd been doing in her job search, as well as for details about her background, before I replied. "There seems to be nothing wrong with what you have to offer to an employer. You're educated, experienced, and have tons of successes under your belt. I see your primary difficulty as being *how* you're job searching, rather than what you have to offer."

Maureen and I talked further, including about how she as a store manager preferred to hire team members. "Did you like running job ads?" Maureen laughed. "No, I *hated* doing that! My desk would get filled with a stack of 100 or more resumes, and then I'd have to sift through them hoping to find a few good people to interview. But I always felt like I was guessing. Plus, it was really expensive to run those ads. I was responsible for the store's bottom line, and after trying that approach a few times, I ditched that strategy. I then started asking my existing team members if they could recommend someone to fill open slots. And occasionally, an ambitious, qualified person would introduce himself to me as a potential employee. I really liked when that happened, because I was always on the lookout for good people. These were much more effective methods than running an ad. I found great people in less time, and it didn't cost me as much."

"So Maureen," I said, looking at her with a twinkle in my eye, "what would make you think that you, an excellent employee, would find a great position through a job ad?" In the next few seconds I could practically see a light bulb turning on in Maureen's mind. "Of course!" she said excitedly. "I need to look at this from the hiring manager's perspective. How do they find the best people? I'm an expert on that! I need to stop wasting my time on these ads!"

I barely had a chance to say goodbye to Maureen as she hurriedly packed up her materials and scooted out of my office. "See you later!" she hollered over her shoulder. "I've got a lot of work to do!"

Core Courage Concept

Connecting with potential employers—whether it's through responding to job ads, approaching companies directly, or hooking up with others to uncover opportunities—takes courage. "Am I good enough?" is a Career Coward's core concern. Afraid of getting burned, job hunters attempt to minimize any potential pain by taking what they believe to be the path of least risk, only applying to job ads. Yet, like the ugly duckling who spends months swimming around with a group of other ducks who don't appreciate him, if you're lucky, you will one day realize that you're swimming with the wrong group of job searchers. You'll then choose to stop putting yourself through such useless pain, and instead get in touch with other swans who can reward you for the valuable contributions you have to offer.

Confidence Checklist

- ☐ Make notes about your current job search process.
- ☐ Compare your activities to the "ideal" job search model.
- ☐ Identify some potential areas for improvement.

Chapter 3

Set a Solid Foundation for Job Search Success

In the last chapter, you identified some specific avenues for improving your search results. From here, we'll work together, step by step, to build a strong base for executing your job search so that you can achieve your desired career goals. We'll start by defining which areas you want to focus on in your search, and then review an estimated job hunting timeline and process, so that you'll know your expected timeframe for success. Here we go!

Risk It or Run From It?

- **Risk Rating: Low to mid-level risk.** Choosing a focus for your job search might make you squirm just a bit, but it's worth it. The "How to Define Your Job Search Focus, Process, and Timeline" section in this chapter is simple to interpret—just read it to easily estimate your own timeframe.

- **Payoff Potential:** Huge beyond words! As many as 95 percent of job searchers don't have a clear focus, and are extremely disappointed with the outcomes of their searches. Those who do have a clear focus achieve better, faster results. You'll be one of them!

(continued)

(continued)

- **Time to Complete:** A few minutes or longer, depending on how much work you might need to do on your focus.

- **Bailout Strategy:** If you're already able to clearly articulate the kind of work you're seeking, as well as the industries that hire for your specialty, feel free to quickly skim through the job search timeline and process section in this chapter before moving on to the next one.

- **The "20 Percent Extra" Edge:** My "Huge beyond words!" comment above wasn't an exaggeration. Taking the time to clearly define the kind of work you're looking for will give you a massive edge, landing you in the top 5–10 percent of most effective job searchers.

- **"Go For It!" Bonus Activity:** Identify up to three focus areas that fit for your career goals. Then complete the suggested activities in this book for all three of your job search focus areas—you'll triple your opportunities and multiply your results.

How to Define Your Job Search Focus, Process, and Timeline

If you like the idea of getting maximum payoff in your job search, with a minimum of wasted time and effort on your part, you'll love this chapter. Read on to discover how to become laser focused to achieve fantastic results.

Identify Your Job Search Focus

My younger sister, Lynn, loves to shop. She will happily devote days and days to walking through stores, and checking out the wares, in hopes of finding great bargains and unique items. Shopping is truly one of her favorite pastimes. Me...I *hate* to shop. I prefer to know exactly what I want, zoom into the store to find and pay for it, and then escape as soon as possible. Our two styles are very different. Hers is broad and leisurely, while mine is focused and fast. We both get the job done, but our timelines and activities are very different.

In my experience, most Career Cowards understand the value of a job search that is focused and fast, as opposed to one that is broad and leisurely. (Unless, of course, you're like my sister and love to devote hours and hours to the hunt!) To accomplish a fast-and-focused search, it's essential that you have a clear picture of what you're aiming for. The following steps will help you define this goal:

- What role are you hoping for in your next position? For instance, do you like to lead groups or functions as a Supervisor, Manager, or Director? Or do you like to execute a specific task, such as an Assembler, Accountant, or Mechanic would do? Or how about monitoring several activities, as a Project Manager, Coordinator, or Organizer might do? Or is it more your style to create products or processes as a Designer, Architect, or Engineer? If you're having trouble articulating your job role, consider these clues:

  - What roles have you been in before that you enjoyed? What were your former position titles, and would you want to find similar work?

  - What skills or talents do you possess that might be translated into a role, such as public speaking (Speaker), teaching (Teacher), or repairing things (Repair Specialist)?

  - What schooling have you received that qualifies you for a particular role? For instance, have you been trained as an Accountant, Massage Therapist, or Counselor?

Aim to identify one to three roles that would be appealing targets for this job search and list those here:

1. _____

2. _____

3. _____

Panic Point! Do you feel as if I'm asking you to put yourself into a box, and you really don't want to be boxed in? I know from experience that *most* Career Cowards don't like to choose a focus for their job search. Like my little sister and her shopping style, they believe that by keeping their job searches broad, they'll eventually run into a position that is unique and special—one that they never would have imagined for themselves before! Yet unlike finding a unique and special pair of shoes, jobs are not lined up on shelves at your favorite department store. Instead, the best positions are most often slightly hidden in the job market, and require a more strategic investigation to uncover.

By deciding on a role (or two or three) for your hunt, you'll be better able to hone in on the opportunities that aren't as obvious. So even if it makes you squirm a bit, do your best to choose a role or two for your search, keeping in mind that you can modify your focus areas later if you choose.

- Which industries are a good fit for the job role you chose? Let's say, for instance, that you love to coordinate activities, projects, and people, so you've chosen "Coordinator" as one of your job roles. Now ask yourself "What do I like about or am I good at with coordinating?" Maybe it's events, or newly engineered products, or marketing campaigns. For ideas on where you might want to apply your job role, flip through the Yellow Pages phone book, asking yourself, "Would I like to be a (Teacher, Manager, Accountant, Lawyer, Coordinator, etc.) in this category? Or this one?" As you flip through the directory, make a list of 10–20 industries that appeal to you. Have fun with this activity…it can open your mind to many possibilities that you might not have considered before!

Panic Point! If you didn't like the idea of choosing a job role, because you felt as if it would box you in, you might dislike the idea of choosing specific industries even more. "I could succeed in *any* industry," you might be thinking. "What's the point of limiting it to just 10 to 20?" While it's true that you might be able to succeed at working in *any* industry, it's nearly impossible to job search effectively in all of them. Again, picture my sister, leisurely driving from store to store, looking for items that catch her eye. She could literally devote every waking hour to this activity. Do you really have the time to do that in your job search, investigating company after company (after company after company...) in hopes of uncovering the one ideal job? My guess is no, you don't have the time or the interest to do that. By identifying 10–20 industries where you'd be most interested in working, you make your search strategy much more effective and achievable. So give it a go—flip through the Yellow Pages and choose some categories that look interesting. You might be surprised to find several that are extremely appealing to you, and that don't make you feel as if I'm trying to box you in.

List your 10–20 Yellow Pages industry categories here:

1. _____

2. _____

3. _____

4. _____

5. _____

6. _____

7. _____

8. _____

9. _____

10. _____

11. _____

12. _____

13. _____

14. _____

15. _____

16. _____

17. _____

18. _____

19. _____

20. _____

Finally, combine your chosen job roles with your selected industries. This is as easy as adding 1 + 2 to get 3. For example, let's say that you've chosen the following job roles:

1. Sales Specialist

2. Marketing Coordinator

3. Event Organizer

...and these industries:

1. Advertising Agencies

2. Day Care Services

3. Recreation Centers

4. Home Furnishings

5. Banks

6. Restaurants

7. Veterinary Clinics

8. Nail Salons

9. Racetracks

10. Radio Stations

To combine them, simply match a job role with an industry, and ask yourself, "Could this combination be an effective job search focus for me?" For instance, consider this partial list of 30 potential combinations created by using the roles and industries mentioned earlier:

- Marketing Coordinator, *Racetracks*

- Sales Specialist, *Radio Stations*

- Event Organizer, *Advertising Agencies*

- Sales Specialist, *Day Care Services*

- Marketing Coordinator, *Banks*

- Event Organizer, *Home Furnishings*

By merging a job role with industries that interest you, you can quickly create a very powerful and appealing focus—one that will help you attain fast and fabulous job search results!

As a final step, write your one to three job search focus areas here:

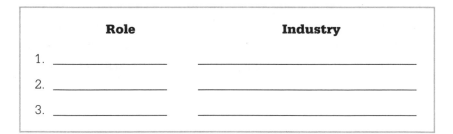

	Role	**Industry**
1.	_____	_____
2.	_____	_____
3.	_____	_____

To make your chosen job search focus areas even more powerful, also define geographically where you'd like to work—such as within 30 minutes of your house, out of a home office, or in another country—as well as how much income you're aiming to earn. Identify as many details about your ideal position as possible. Down the line, this vision will allow you to develop and execute a more successful search plan.

If you're feeling confused and lost about choosing a job search focus, check out *The Career Coward's Guide to Changing Careers* for additional ideas and effective strategies for defining a job search role that fits your unique skills, talents, and interests.

Estimate How Long Your Job Search Will Take

A few years back, I needed a root canal on a tooth that was causing me trouble. As you might imagine, I was pretty anxious about the process. Finally the dreaded day arrived, and I found myself lying in the dentist's chair, sweating over what would happen next. But instead of beginning her drilling immediately, the endodontist took a few minutes to describe the steps she would take to complete the root canal, and about how long the entire process would take (less than an hour). Then, once she began, I had some idea of what she was doing. I also kept an eye on the clock, telling myself, "Just 30 minutes more…just 15 minutes more…" and so on. Because she had given me a clear idea of what to expect, I felt more in control of what was happening. And when it was finally over, I realized it wasn't as awful as I'd expected it would be.

The purpose of this section is similar to what my endodontist provided for me with my root canal: It helps you to understand an estimated timeframe for your job search and approximately how long each step will take. The following chart of activities will help you calculate an estimated timeline:

Job Search Process Step	Estimated Timeline
Decide on a focus for your job search	*A few minutes or longer.* Hopefully, you've already completed this step in the process, using the strategy defined in this chapter.

Job Search Process Step	**Estimated Timeline**
Identify and research a list of potential employers.	*A few hours to a few days*, depending on how much time you want to put into your research. We'll begin this process in chapter 4.
Develop effective job search tools.	*A few days to a week* to create cover letters, resumes, and other job search tools that will support your effective search. In chapters 5 and 6 we'll cover these steps.
Implement your job search activities.	*One month for every $10,000 you expect to earn in your next position.* Over a period of weeks, you will be submitting applications, approaching employers directly, networking with helpful supporters, and interviewing for positions. One helpful (and fairly accurate!) guideline is to estimate one month of job searching for every $10,000 you can expect to earn in the position(s) you're targeting. For instance, if you can anticipate earning approximately $50,000 as an Accountant for a computer manufacturing company, your search should take about five months to complete.

An estimated timeline for your successful job search will be:

Why It's Worth Doing

Colin Frager, one of the nation's most effective executive recruiters, occasionally shares his insights with me regarding effective job search. One of my all-time favorite comments from him is, "Of all the job searchers who contact me, only about 5 percent of them have a clear idea for what they want in their next position. My job as a recruiter is to put square-peg candidates into square holes, and round-peg candidates into round holes. If a candidate doesn't know what kind of peg he is, I certainly don't have the time to help him figure it out."

Over the years, assisting thousands of job hunters, I've learned that Frager's mindset runs counter to how most job searchers think. Whereas Frager's opinion is, "Know what you want, so that I can help plug you into the right hole," most job searchers prefer to think, "I'll mold myself to fit any sized hole, provided it looks interesting enough."

On paper, the "mold me" mindset would seem to work, because it allows for greater flexibility. However, in reality, most job searchers don't have extensive periods of time to check into thousands of businesses seeking out potential positions—in whatever form they might take. Even more important, most employers don't have the time (or interest!) to determine whether a job hunter would be a fit for his or her needs. Rather than, "Can I use you?" busy decision makers are asking, "What can you do for me?" For these reasons, being able to say, "I'm seeking an X position in the Y industry," allows people like Frager, as well as hiring managers and other supporters in your job search, to help you most effectively.

By choosing a job search focus (or two or three), made up of a specific role combined with a particular industry, you will be able to move forward more easily and effectively in your search.

Career Champ Profile: Andre

Andre, a 50-something job searcher, came to see me for suggestions on how to improve his results. He had been hunting unsuccessfully for eight months and was hungry for new ideas and approaches.

"What kind of work are you aiming for," I asked. "That's the problem," he began. "I can do so many things. I've headed a manufacturing division, been project manager in technical product development, and handled supply chain logistics for companies. I like lots of challenge and would rather not pigeonhole myself into something too narrow. A really exciting opportunity might exist out there—something I've never even considered before—and I want to keep myself open for it."

I asked him to tell me about the job search processes he'd been using so far. "Mostly finding and applying to jobs on the Internet. In particular, I watch websites advertising jobs with technical companies." I then asked the famous Dr. Phil question, "How's that working for you?"

"Not so good," Andre confessed. "I'm getting very few responses to my applications, and I'm feeling pretty frustrated."

"Okay, how about this," I offered. "Let's experiment with some different approaches to see if we can boost your results. To begin, let's have you pick just three job search focus areas, made up of specific job titles and industries." I could tell by the look on Andre's face that he wasn't thrilled with my suggestion. "Keep in mind that we can change or add to the job search focus areas you choose. This is just a place to start."

"Well, my job search strategies aren't working so great, so I guess it's worth it to try your way for a while," he conceded.

Over the next few weeks Andre narrowed his job search focus down to three areas: Project Manager for high-tech R&D firms, Quality Manager for mid-sized manufacturing businesses, and Supply Chain Specialist within high-, mid-, and low-tech manufacturing companies. He also customized a resume for each of these focus areas, highlighting the experiences and training he possessed that were most relevant, and researching a list of 100 potential employers in the industry segments that he'd identified. Then Andre launched a new-and-improved job search campaign, applying to advertised jobs, approaching his target companies directly, and networking with contacts connected to his target companies and industries.

In less than a month, Andre's search took a turn for the better. He started getting requests for interviews from recruiters and hiring managers. He was able to network more often and more easily with helpful contacts at his target companies, helping him to feel more connected and energized in his job search. And within four months, Andre landed an offer for a $90,000 per year Project Manager position with an R&D firm.

Core Courage Concept

Being willing to clearly state what kind of position you're seeking, and setting aside (even temporarily) other job search focus areas, takes a great deal of courage, especially for Career Cowards. Although you could maintain a broad search approach, keeping yourself open to whatever might cross your path, the results could be long and frustrating. Instead, just as you can aim light through a magnifying glass to achieve fast, effective results, you can get your search smoking quickly by defining a job search focus that's right for you.

Confidence Checklist

☐ Identify your job search focus.

☐ Estimate how long your job search will take.

Chapter 4

Find Out Where You Fit

How would it feel to know that 20, 100, or even more companies are a great match for your talents and experience—and that with just a little bit of research, you could identify these companies and begin to connect with them to uncover great job opportunities? If this sounds good to you, read on to find out how to locate and learn about a wealth of potential employers just right for your career goals.

Risk It or Run From It?

- **Risk Rating:** Very low. Although this step might feel like a lot of work, there's not much danger involved—just time and effort.

- **Payoff Potential:** This is one of those super-high-payoff (yet very low-risk) activities. It's a definite "must do!"

- **Time to Complete:** It might take you a few hours—but they would be a few of the most valuable hours you devote to your job search.

- **Bailout Strategy:** Hmmmmmm…. The target list is so important, I'm not sure you'll want to bail on this step. How about a quick-and-dirty shortcut? At the minimum, look

(continued)

(continued)

> through the relevant industry categories in your Yellow Pages and make a list of 20 or more potential employers. Or hire someone else to do the research for you.
>
> - **The "20 Percent Extra" Edge:** Having a clear picture of where you fit in the job market allows you to connect faster, and more successfully, with potential employers.
>
> - **"Go For It!" Bonus Activity:** Skip ahead to chapter 10 to find out how to organize the company information you collect, so that you can be more effective even faster!

How to Scope Out a Long List of Potential Employers

In my work, I've had thousands of conversations similar to this one:

Job Searcher: "There are just no jobs out there that fit my interests and skills. It's very discouraging."

Me: "How have you been job searching?"

Job Searcher: "I watch the newspaper ads, of course. And there are a number of Internet job sites that I check regularly."

Me: "Do you have a target list of 20–100 employers that would be likely to hire someone with your background, and who you'd be interested in working for?"

Job Searcher: "Weeeeeelllllll, I have a list of places where I've sent my resume. Is that the same thing?"

Me: "Not exactly. Creating a target list would most likely be an effective, confidence-building activity for you. It would help you find many more opportunities that are a good fit for your interests and skills. Want to learn more?"

Job Searcher: "Sure, especially if it will lead to more good jobs for me!"

If this sounds a little like a conversation you and I might have if we were talking, read on to learn more about target lists and how they can benefit your job search.

Brainstorm What Types of Organizations Match Your Job Search Focus

Congratulations! In the last chapter, you defined your job search focus, a step that will make finding an awesome position so much easier. Now we're going to use that focus to your best advantage. To begin, write your focus information below:

I am searching for a position where I will potentially serve in these roles:

1) _____   2) _____ 3) _____

...possibly in these industries:

1) _____   2) _____ 3) _____

Now, to brainstorm your target list of potential employers, we're going to focus primarily on the industries you just listed. Let's say, for example, that you have identified the following job search focus roles and industries:

I am searching for a position where I will potentially serve in these roles:

1) Event Coordinator 2) Account Manager 3) Customer
                                        Service Specialist

...potentially in these industries:

1) Hotels and Resorts 2) Event Supply Centers
3) Nonprofit Agencies

Paying attention to the industries portion of your job search focus, you'll now want to define these fields a bit more to help you develop a solid, productive list of target employers.

Let's take Hotels and Resorts, for example. Which segments of this category are most interesting to you? Take a minute to consider what you'd *truly* hope for in terms of the nature of work and environments you'd like to be connected to. Do you have more of an interest in bed and breakfasts? Spas? Large, posh hotels? Which specific areas best fit your interests? It might help to flip through the appropriate categories in your Yellow Pages directory for ideas.

When you've finished defining your industry categories in more detail, your list might look something like this:

- Hotels and Resorts: Bed and Breakfasts, Retreat Centers, Inns

- Event Supply Centers: Caterers, Party Rental Centers

- Nonprofit Agencies: Children's Services, Housing Support, Arts

Panic Point! Are you thinking, "I really don't *care* which industry I work for. I just want a job!" Or, "My specialty can fit into pretty much any industry. Why should I limit myself to only a few types of businesses?" If either of these statements is true for you, consider this: The purpose of defining a list of industries and businesses is primarily *to help you job search more effectively.* It will be much *easier* for you to uncover interesting, great-fit positions if you have a defined number of places to look. If you don't like the idea of defining potential employers by industry, use another criteria—geography, for example, and identify businesses within a certain distance from your home. But I highly recommend having some kind of defining criteria. Otherwise, you'd need to investigate hundreds or thousands of potential employers, rather than just 20 to 100. Your search would be so broad and scattered that you'd wind up frustrated, with poor results. I don't want that for you! Go ahead and define a list of potential employers. It will significantly contribute to your success in the long run. I promise!

Got your initial categories defined? Good for you! You're well on your way to developing a valuable, productive target list. Now you can move on to the next step.

Develop Lists of Potential Employers

Since you've already chosen your sorting criteria, this next step should be easy-sneezy. Now it's time for you to develop a list of specific employers that fall within the categories you've selected. As you do so, keep in mind that it's wise to list small- and medium-sized employers, as well as larger, more well-known companies. Why? Because most of us—about 75 percent, in fact—work for organizations with fewer than 25 employees, so it makes sense to factor in some smaller companies. Following are some resources to help you build your target list.

- **Yellow Pages:** Yes, the good ole Yellow Pages. You can make use of either the hardcopy or Internet version; however, an Internet Yellow Pages directory offers some real advantages. Often, these sites will automatically suggest other categories for you to consider (such as, if you picked "Jewelry," they might also suggest "Accessories" or "Antiques"). And these sites will often provide links to company Web pages, making it easy for you to gather additional information about an organization.

- **Directories:** Several useful directories and registers exist to help you in compiling your list of target companies. Many are free or are very moderately priced. For instance, in northern Colorado, where I live, job searchers can obtain lists of companies using the Northern Colorado Business Report's *Book of Lists* or one of its many other industry-specific directories (it publishes medical, technology, agricultural, and construction versions). Your city might offer helpful resources like this also, for purchase or for use at your area library. One significant advantage to using local directories is that they often provide information about smaller organizations that might not be included in national databases. Professional groups and associations might also be a great resource. Call or stop by your library's reference desk for ideas and to learn which directories might be available and useful to you.

- **Databases:** Similar to directories, a wide range of electronic databases exist to help you research organizations for your target company list. My local library, for example, offers access to Reference USA, a database of businesses in the United States, which can be accessed online or by using one of the computers at the library. This database (as most do) allows you to obtain lists of companies by industry, using a coding system such as the NAICS (North American Industrial Classification System). Several other company databases can be accessed online as well.

Developing your target list can be a fun, fast, rewarding activity. For instance, using the categories I just defined, and researching organizations using www.dexknows.com (my regional Yellow Pages Web site), I came up with a list of 200+ businesses in just five minutes of searching. And there's a wonderful bonus that comes along with researching company names: You'll very quickly see that there are many more potential employers and opportunities out there than you realized before. This can be a *huge* boost to a Career Coward's motivation!

Compile Powerful Profiles of Your Target Companies

Wow…now you're really on your way. You've selected a job search focus, and begun building your list of target companies. As a final step in this process, you'll collect important details about each of your target organizations to help launch your search successfully. For the companies on your list, aim to gather the following information:

- Organization name
- Address

- Phone, e-mail

- Summary of the organization's purpose, mission, products, and services

- Details about the business's customers

- Key decision makers in the company, particularly those related to your specialty (such as the Director of Sales, if you're seeking a position as a sales representative)

- Bonus Information — Recent announcements provided on the company's Web page, or through news sources, such as newspapers

Panic Point! Are you feeling overwhelmed with the amount of information you'll need to gather? I don't blame you! You're not the first job searcher to feel this way. In fact, most job searchers quit at this point. It takes discipline to pull together all of these details, and most people just aren't willing to do it. Plus you might be asking yourself, "Is it really worth it?" Here's the scoop: Each piece of information you collect is one more brick in the foundation of your solid job search. The data you gather will help you present yourself more successfully to potential employers, giving you a *huge* advantage over your competition. So yes, it's worth it to gather all of this data about your target companies. Just keep nudging yourself to take tiny steps forward. Pick an organization that seems especially interesting to you as a place to start. You'll most likely discover that gathering the info doesn't take that much time or effort, and might actually be fun.

Let's say that you want to gather information about my business, Career Solutions Group. How would you do it? A company name search on www.google.com is a good place to start. From there, you could then log on to my Web page to gather most of the following information.

- Organization name: Career Solutions Group

- Address: 430 Stover Street, Fort Collins, CO, 80524, USA

- Phone, e-mail: (970) 224-4042, www.careersolutionsgroup.net, katy@careersolutionsgroup.net

- Summary of the organization's purpose, mission, products, and services: Empowering career-minded individuals to achieve meaningful, satisfying career goals through fun, effective, and accessible products and services, such as career counseling, resume development, interview preparation, and job search assistance.

- Details about the business's customers: Career changers, job searchers, and companies needing outplacement support for transitioning employees.

- Key decision makers in the company, particularly those related to your specialty: Katy Piotrowski, Career Counselor.

- Bonus Information—Recent announcements provided on the company's Web page, or through news sources, such as newspapers: Katy has just released a new book in the *Career Coward's* series.

In total, aim to compile a list of 25–100 potential employers, researching as many key pieces of information as you can. Your target list will be one of your most valuable job search tools.

Why It's Worth Doing

I'll admit it right up front: This step—developing a list of target employers—is one that is especially difficult for me to nudge Career Cowards to do. Creating a list of target employers is hard, tedious work. So why don't I just give up on nagging job searchers to do it? *Because this single activity can make the difference between conducting a job search that is energizing and successful, or one that is a disappointing failure.* Yes, it's *that* important.

Still not convinced? Well, consider it from this perspective: When they're job hunting, most people (about 90 percent of them) will only pay attention to jobs that are clearly advertised as being open. And, as a result, they *only* look at companies who announce positions this way. However, about 70 percent of businesses (the majority of them!) *never* advertise openings. They fill them through better, higher quality avenues. So unless you strategically research a list of organizations that interest you, you might never learn about businesses that would benefit from having you join their teams, plus you run the risk of missing out on 70 percent of the job opportunities that are available! So is it worth it to spend a few hours developing a list of target companies? You decide.

Career Champ Profile: Sid

Sid looked at me with mock anger. "Why didn't you force me to do this company research exercise *earlier* in my job search? It would have completely changed how I was going about things. These companies that I've researched in the last week seem *so* much more interesting to me than the businesses where I've replied to job ads."

For the last three months, Sid had been searching for a position as a Human Resources Specialist. But there hadn't been many HR jobs advertised, so he'd been applying to administrative, customer service, and office support positions as well.

Yet when he finally decided to research a list of target companies—an activity Sid learned about early in his search, but didn't try right away (I still haven't discovered a way to *force* my clients to try what I recommend!)—Sid discovered a world of companies he'd never considered before, businesses that seemed to be a much better match for his personal interests.

"See, look at this company," Sid said, pulling out a printout of a company Web page. "This business is developing wind-energy products. They're helping to reduce pollution. That's so cool! And I don't even care that they don't have a specific position open. I'm contacting them anyway. I have great things to offer a company like this, and I want to make sure they know about me."

Over the next few weeks, Sid added to his database of information about target companies, locating more and more organizations that looked intriguing to him, and contacting them to learn about potential openings. The data he collected renewed his motivation for finding a great-fitting position...and not long after that, he did!

Core Courage Concept

In some ways, it can feel safer not to get too specific about what you really want in a career opportunity. Subconsciously, many Career Cowards believe that if they don't put too much hope into defining what they truly want, they won't be as disappointed if it doesn't happen. But does life really work this way? You can most likely answer this for yourself. Which technique has worked better for you: articulating details about your hopes and dreams, or vaguely wishing for something better? For most people (especially Career Cowards) putting in the time and effort to define what they want—such as developing a list of target employers—is a much more effective technique. Yes, it might seem tedious and overwhelming at first, but you *can* do it...and you'll be much better off for the effort.

Confidence Checklist

- [ ] Brainstorm what types of organizations match your job search focus.
- [ ] Develop lists of potential employers.
- [ ] Compile powerful profiles of your target companies.

Part 2

Implement a Successful (and Fearless) Search Strategy

Chapter 5

Build a Confident Resume

A long time ago, when my grandmother was a young house-wife, she took a class that showed her how to make a sewing center. It was a freestanding, two-sided unit, about waist high, built of wood and fabric. The inside was lined with many pockets, designed to hold her sewing tools and materials.

As a child, I used to look at that sewing center with awe. She would let me take out and play with the buttons, lace, thread, scissors, patches, and needles. The idea of repairing a sock using her darning egg, or digging through her button bag to find just the right one, made the task of sewing seem like a joy, rather than a chore.

Having the right tools—organized and at your fingertips—can make the difference between completing a task easily and struggling each step of the way. In this chapter, we'll focus on creating one of your most powerful job search tools: your resume.

Risk It or Run From It?

- **Risk Rating:** Creating a resume can feel like a huge risk to many job searchers. Yet in reality, there's very little risk in the actual process of creating one. Down the line, when it comes time to launch your resume into the job market, the risk will

(continued)

(continued)

rise. But for now, you're still out of the danger zone, so just take a deep breath and keep moving forward.

- **Payoff Potential:** An effective resume can be one of your most essential tools in a successful job search. It's worth the effort it takes to create one.

- **Time to Complete:** A few hours.

- **Bailout Strategy:** You can always hire someone to write your resume for you. A professionally produced resume is an excellent investment. Or you might already have a resume you like. If so, skim through the "Put Your Resume to the Test" criteria later in this chapter to make sure it's producing the results you deserve. If so, feel free to move on to the next chapter.

- **The "20 Percent Extra" Edge:** On average, a "typical" resume will generate a call for an interview about 10 percent of the time. Yet a strong resume will result in calls for interviews 50 percent or more of the time. Having a strong resume in your job hunting toolbox will go a long way toward speeding up your search.

- **"Go For It!" Bonus Activity:** After you create your resume, run it by three or four people who have experience hiring people for your specialty and ask them for suggestions on improving it.

How to Create a Resume That Generates Positive Results

There are as many ways to create a resume as there are people. Following are some proven successful suggestions for creating powerful resumes that help you achieve your job search goals, along with two resume examples demonstrating the techniques described. As you read through the following ideas, keep in mind that there's no one "right" way to create a resume. As long as your resume generates interviews, it's working! And if you're looking for thousands of other great tips for creating effective resumes, check out *The Career Coward's Guide to Resumes* by yours truly.

Clearly State Your Objective

Over the last several years of helping clients create resumes, I've discovered that the objective is a highly debated part of the document. Some people feel very strongly that it's better to not include an objective, so their resumes are more flexible for a variety of opportunities. Other people believe that an objective helps resume screeners quickly determine whether each candidates' career goal matches their needs.

I strongly believe in the value of including an objective, primarily because I've discovered that resumes that clearly state and support a specific career goal produce a significantly higher rate of interviews than those that don't. For this reason, I recommend that you build an objective into each resume, using one of the following strategies:

- Use the job title provided in a job ad. For instance, if the position description is entitled "Customer Care Representative," adopt that as your objective.

- Create a job title that fits the types of positions for which you're aiming. And guess what…you've already done this step! Simply include the role (and industry, too, if it makes sense) that you defined for your job search objective in chapter 3.

Include Keywords to Boost Your Resume's Results

Adding in keywords—the phrasing and terminology included in job descriptions to describe position requirements—will increase the chances of your resume being selected from among the many other resumes that have been submitted for an opening. This is because often computer programs sort submitted resumes using keywords as a filter. Lucky for you, it's easy to add keywords to your resume. These techniques produce excellent results:

- Copy and paste phrasing from a job ad directly into your resume; and then modify the verbiage to accurately represent your background.

- Collect several keywords that pertain to your job search focus by reviewing a number of job ads off of a search site such as www.monster.com. Synthesize these phrases into a paragraph of keywords to include.

Format Your Work History, Experience, and Education to Best Support Your Job Search Goals

Resumes can be organized in several ways. Two of the most popular formats are chronological and functional/skill-based (see the examples included figures 5.1 and 5.2). In general, it makes sense to use a chronological format resume if you're aiming to stay within, or progress further in, your current career. This is because a chronological format allows you to show progression and commitment to a chosen specialty. However, if you're making a career change, or are new to or reentering the workforce, a functional resume is most likely the best choice for you because it is set up to highlight the details about you that are most relevant to your career goal.

For further ideas on how to present your work history, experiences, and education, see the resume samples in this chapter, as well as those presented in *The Career Coward's Guide to Resumes*.

Put Your Resume to the Test

Once you've created a resume, you can determine its effectiveness using the following success criteria:

- Within 10 seconds or less, is a reader of your resume able to gain a clear idea of the kind of position you're aiming for, as well as a few key pieces of information about your qualifications?

- Does your resume consistently generate a fair rate of interviews for you? For instance, one interview for every 10 resumes submitted is an average result, so your resume should achieve this or even better.

- Is your resume easily customizable, allowing you to tweak it quickly to take advantage of opportunities?

If you can answer "Yes!" to these three questions, your resume is a strong tool for your job search toolbox. If not, consider reworking and enhancing your resume to achieve better results.

Carolyn Marinson   *Elementary Teacher*

724 Windmill Drive
Fort Collins, CO 80524
970-222-3333, carolyn14@aol.com

Experienced, knowledgeable Elementary Teacher with 5+ years of background teaching grade-school students. Adept at applying teaching principles and methods for curriculum development and successful student learning. Able to adapt teaching techniques used to support students' individual differences in ability, personality, and interests. Excel at establishing and maintaining respectful relationships with students, parents, and co-workers. Able to monitor educational development and administer tests to evaluate and increase student performance.

EDUCATION & LICENSURE

> **B.A., Interdisciplinary Studies with emphasis in Elementary Education**
>
> Fort Timber College, 2006

> **Colorado Teacher's License** grades K–6

> **First Aid and CPR Certified**

TEACHING EXPERIENCE

Teacher (substitute), <u>Grades K–6</u>, 2006–Present   *Platte School District*

- Effectively deliver instruction, per teachers' plans, in a range of elementary school environments:

  > **Coordinate with teachers to deliver quality instruction to students using appropriate classroom materials and techniques.**

  > Maintain documentation when needed to capture students' pertinent academic, social, and emotional needs.

- Effectively communicate students' progress and needs with teachers and staff, and collaborate with instructors and departments through meetings and discussions.

Student Teacher, <u>First Grade</u>, Fall 2006   *Louden Elementary*

- Taught students and worked with grade-level teaching team to ensure successful achievement of learning objectives.

  > **Applied effective classroom-management techniques to achieve a successful, respectful learning environment.**

- Coordinated student material development with instructor, and acquired valuable student-records-management experience.

- Worked with special projects teams within the school to improve overall quality and results.

Full-Time Student, Elementary Education, 2002–2006   *Fort Timber College*

- Successfully completed numerous courses addressing the latest advances and techniques in effective elementary school education.

- Consistently achieved high grades and positive feedback from instructors and classmates.

Figure 5.1: Chronological resume example.

Len McCarthy   *Account Management*
3502 Mountain Creek Drive
Fort Collins, CO 80528
970-222-9999, lmcarthy@email.com

Highly motivated, results-oriented Sales Account Manager with proven success in building productive client relationships and delivering quality products and services. Possess strengths in successfully expanding sales territories and meeting quotas. Knowledgeable in identifying target markets and implementing new revenue streams. Strategic at building, motivating, and leading teams to achieve goals. Skilled at problem solving and creative thinking. Offer outstanding communications and team-building expertise.

PROFESSIONAL EXPERIENCE & ACCOMPLISHMENTS

- o   **Account Manager/Broker,** *Warm Hearth Residential Brokerage,* 2006–Present
- o   **Customer Development Manager,** *Advantage Enterprises,* 2005–2006
- o   **Director, GM/HBC Department,** *Advantage Enterprises,* 2001–2005
- o   **Business Manager,** *MBC Inc.* 1997–2001

Account Management Expertise

- Able to create and implement strategic sales programs to build sales and achieve customer satisfaction.
- Offer proven results in strategically expanding sales territories and increasing business revenue.
  - o   **Supervised sales team, customer service representatives, merchandisers, and managers, resulting in $98M sales generation to major grocery chains and wholesalers.**
  - o   **Managed $25M sales territory while consistently meeting or exceeding quotas.**
- Adept at successfully maintaining accounts while developing new prospects within a territory.
  - o   **Managed corporate food and drug retail accounts for consumer products to major grocery retailers in southern California.**
- Possess outstanding track record for establishing positive rapport with prospects through trade show, training seminar, office visit, and conference call venues.

Business Leadership Experience

- Skilled at identifying and implementing marketing programs to enhance sales and grow business.
- Adept at managing and motivating teams in order to attain organizational objectives.
  - o   **Supervised, educated, and grew a staff of 8 retail sales representatives, successfully sustaining an existing client base, while growing territories and expanding sales and profits.**
- Knowledgeable in negotiating contracts and maintaining current-payment status with customers.

EDUCATION & TRAINING

- o   **Bachelor of Science, Business Management,** California State Polytechnic University
- o   **Associate of Arts, Humanities,** Cerritos College
- o   **Sergeant,** United States Army

Figure 5.2: Functional resume example.

Why It's Worth Doing

I probably don't need to convince you that a resume is an essential tool in job searching. However, you might not yet realize the importance of preparing targeted resumes that clearly support your job search goals.

Over the years, I've looked at thousands of resumes, and talked with just about that many job searchers. In most cases (70 percent, I'd guesstimate), the job hunter's resume *doesn't* clearly reflect his or her job search goals. Consequently, the job seeker's results are disappointing, and major opportunities are missed.

Investing the time and energy necessary to create a powerful, focused resume can significantly improve your job search results and open doors that allow you to attain your career goals.

Career Champ Profile: Jonah

After being laid off from his position as a drafter/designer, Jonah took a job as a cab driver, eager to spend his days doing work that was less stressful and more predictable. This strategy worked well for a few years, but then Jonah found himself missing the creativity and challenge of drafting and design, so he decided to search for a position that would allow him to do that kind of work once again.

Putting together his resume seemed to present a problem, however. How could Jonah account for his last few years of work history as a cab driver, yet still present a solid picture of his skills and experience within design and drafting? Ultimately Jonah opted to present his information using a functional resume format, allowing him to clearly state his job search objective, include keywords pertinent to the positions he was targeting, and present his work history, experiences, and education in a format that highlighted his relevant skills as a designer/drafter. Figure 5.3 is the result, which supported Jonah's job search goals very well.

Jonah Blade   *Mechanical Design Drafter*
1006 Spring Climb Ct.
Fort Collins, CO 80526
970-2222-8888, jblade@comcast.net

Highly motivated and skilled **Mechanical Design Drafter** with broad knowledge of design and manufacturing. Able to save time and money through interpreting and applying user and company design requirements and distilling them into successful design solutions. Adept at leveraging existing data into new designs. Skilled in use of CAD. Offer excellent interpersonal and organizational skills to ensure timely, on-budget completion of projects.

WORK HISTORY

- **Mechanical Design Drafter,** *Amber Technologies / ICA,* 2+ years
- **Mechanical Design Drafter,** *JB Design,* 5 years
- **Assoc. Prof. Mechanical Design/Drafting,** *AimHigh Community College,* 4 years
- **Customer Service,** *ServicePro Dial a Ride,* 2005–Present
- **Team Lead/Customer Service Agent,** *Business Plus,* 2001–2005
  Additional drafting and design experience available upon request

DESIGN & DRAFTING EXPERIENCE

- Highly knowledgeable and skilled drafter and CAD technician.
  - o **Never missed a deadline due to lack of skill on a CAD platform.**
  - o **Praised by superiors for technical competence.**
- Adept at capturing and conveying engineer's design intent.
  - o **Specifically sought out by engineers and project managers to work on more complex design projects.**
- Able to collect, analyze, and distill data from stakeholders into accurate designs, parts, and assemblies.
  - o **Developed reputation for doing the job right the first time, leading to increasing responsibility for projects.**
- Possess strong interpersonal and communication skills coupled with broad and deep knowledge of design and manufacturing processes.
  - o **Successfully led cross-functional teams to develop branding and usability guidelines for business group.**
  - o **Promoted to Industrial Design Program Manager.**
- Offer strengths in collaborating with project managers, R&D engineers, manufacturing engineers, and others to develop designs and resolve problems.
  - o **Designed and developed an engineering prototype for a new electronic enclosure on time and on budget.**

EDUCATION & TECHNICAL SKILLS

- Bachelor of Fine Arts, Cum Laude, Michigan State University
- Office Software: MS Word, Excel, PowerPoint, Outlook, Project
- CAD Programs: Microstation, Solid Designer, AutoCAD, Solidworks

---

Figure 5.3: Jonah's functional resume.

Core Courage Concept

Clearly stating your job search goals on your resume, and articulating the specific expertise you have to offer, is a lot more difficult than simply putting words on paper. For Career Cowards especially, the true challenge in creating a targeted resume is in admitting what you want to pursue in your career and stating it in black and white for the world to see. But once you take this important step, chances are that you'll believe even more strongly that it's worth it for you to move ahead to accomplishing your job search goals.

Confidence Checklist

- ☐ Clearly state your objective.
- ☐ Include keywords to boost your resume's results.
- ☐ Format your work history, experience, and education to best support your job search goals.
- ☐ Put your resume to the test.

Chapter 6

Create Easy Cover Letters That Get Great Results

You've probably heard the story of the guy who visits his doctor complaining of pain in his eye every time he drinks hot cocoa. After asking a few questions, the doc offers this solution: "Take the spoon out of your cup when you drink." When it comes to creating cover letters, I've observed that most job searchers (Career Cowards especially) make the process much more painful than it needs to be. In this chapter, I'll show you how to "take the spoon out of your cup" to easily create effective cover letters that get great results.

Risk It or Run From It?

- **Risk Rating:** Pretty low. This step-by-step formula will take the guesswork—and the risk—out of the process.

- **Payoff Potential:** High. Cover letters are an expected part of job hunting. By mastering some simple techniques for building them, you'll significantly improve the effectiveness of your search.

- **Time to Complete:** After you learn the steps, a cover letter should take you just 10–30 minutes to create.

(continued)

(continued)

- **Bailout Strategy:** You could use "generic" cover letters, rather than customize one for each opportunity. It would save you some time and brainpower. I don't recommend this approach, however. Sending generic letters runs the risk of your being perceived as someone who doesn't really care about the opportunity.

- **The "20 Percent Extra" Edge:** A strong, concise cover letter immediately tells the decision maker that you're a candidate worth considering!

- **"Go For It!" Bonus Activity:** Research examples of cover letters in sample books and online, and create a file of good ideas to use for yourself.

How to Write Simple, Effective Cover Letters

Several years ago, I worked with a client who had experienced a head injury. Until that time, he'd had a highly successful career in sales. After his accident, however, he lost the ability to write more than a sentence or two. He hired me to help him with his job search...specifically, to write cover letters to submit with his resume to positions of interest.

He was highly motivated to get back to work, and he requested that I prepare 20 or more cover letters for him each week. When we began working together, the thought of writing so many letters seemed overwhelming to me. Yet within a few days of creating his letters, I'd discovered a method for writing a very effective, customized cover letter in about three minutes, and my client received calls for interviews for about 25 percent of the applications he submitted. Since that time, I've stuck with this cover letter writing system.

Set Up Your Letter Professionally

Your cover letter and resume go hand in hand in representing you as a qualified candidate. For this reason, it's important to present your cover letter as professionally as you do your resume. Often, you can easily create your header by copying and pasting the header from your resume. Be sure to include your name or initials, as well as your phone number and e-mail information. Your address is optional, especially if you want to maintain your confidentiality; however, if you don't include your address, at least include some regional information. Here's an example:

D.M.
Northern Colorado
(970) 222-8989
dm32@gmail.com

Enter the Date and Employer Info (Including a Contact Name If Possible)

The type of information you include in the employer's address and your salutation will depend on the opportunity. For instance, if you're responding to a blind ad, it's likely that you won't have a contact name or address. In this case, just list the information you *do* have, such as, "Attention Human Resources, RE: Accounting Specialist Position."

If it's not a blind ad, and a company name or address is provided, I encourage you to research more details about the company using the Internet, or by calling the company directly, aiming to find out the name of the hiring manager.

> **Note:** Unless you're applying for a position within the human resources department, the human resources manager is not the *hiring manager*. The hiring manager is the person you would report to...in other words, your future boss. Although it makes sense to submit your application materials to human resources, it's also highly effective to

(continued)

(continued)

> send a second copy of your materials to the hiring manager. Including the name (properly spelled, of course!) of this person can go a long way toward helping your application materials to stand out from the competition. A quick call to the company asking, "Who is in charge of the *X* department," (filling in the *X* with the function appropriate to your job search focus) is often all it takes to get this valuable piece of data. If you're not able to obtain the name of a contact person, the greeting, "Dear Hiring Manager" is sufficient.

Begin Your Letter with a To-the-Point First Paragraph

The following starter paragraph, customized with specifics relevant to your opportunity, is a great way to begin your letter.

> I am writing to introduce myself and to apply to the JOB TITLE position currently open within your company. Your organization's focus on FILL IN A BRIEF STATEMENT ABOUT ITS PRODUCTS, SERVICES, AND MISSION is of high interest to me, and a good fit for my career focus and background. Following is a summary of my qualifications as they pertain to your position requirements:

Additionally, as you will see in the Career Champ cover letter included in this chapter, if you have the name of a mutual acquaintance who has referred you, the first paragraph is the ideal place to include this information.

List Three Bullets Highlighting the Most Important Aspects of Your Background

For the main part of your cover letter, choose three pieces of information about you that are most relevant to the company's priorities, and highlight them with bullets. Often, you can determine its primary needs from the job ad, or based on your own knowledge of the position. For instance, let's say that the position description listed,

"Experience supporting customers in a fast-paced environment." In response, you could include a bullet such as this:

- *Regarding my ability to support customers in a fast-paced environment, my background includes five years of successful experience providing quality customer service in high-pressure situations. Feedback from my customers and management team about my results in this area has been excellent, including consistently earning top ratings on my performance reviews, and receiving numerous letters of appreciation from the customers I have supported.*

Panic Point! Worried about choosing the "right" three points to cover with your bullet statements? Try not to sweat this step too much. Just pick the three that you feel are most important, *and resist the urge to address* every-thing *about your background in the cover letter.* It's too much for the hiring manager or resume screener to wade through! (Never lose sight of the fact that screeners might be reviewing 100 or more applications...make their jobs easy for them!) Instead, aim to "tease" the reader with a few highlights and then refer them to your resume for more details.

Conclude Your Letter with Proposed Next Steps

Now that the resume screener is excited about what you have to offer based on the three highlighted bullet statements you provided, tell him what you aim to have happen next—specifically, to review your resume, have you in for an interview, or to expect your call:

Additional details about my background are provided on the enclosed resume. I would welcome the opportunity to talk with you further about the JOB TITLE position and how I might benefit your organization in this role. In the next few days, I will follow up with you to confirm receipt of these materials, and to determine a logical next step.

P.S....Finish Strong!

You're in the home stretch now, and need only to finalize your letter with a few closing elements: a classic, "Sincerely" or "Best regards," your signature (if you're submitting hardcopy materials), and possibly a postscript. Savvy marketers know that a P.S. is one of the most widely read parts of a letter, and might offer the ideal opportunity for you to communicate something especially important about your background. Here's an example:

P.S. I read a recent article in the *Times Daily* about your move into South American markets. Please note on my resume that I speak fluent Spanish, and I assisted my last employer with a similar market expansion, with excellent results.

Panic Point! You might be thinking, "This cover letter format seems too 'light.' Shouldn't I be including statements about my character, such as my work ethic and loyalty?" Good question, and the answer is...in general, no. Why? Because it's very difficult to describe your positive qualities in a few sentences and have them come across clearly and sincerely. (Be honest...you've tried this before, haven't you? And it most likely didn't go well.) For example, consider the statement, "I am a hard worker and devoted to going the extra mile to get the job done." Most people, when they read a statement like this, think to themselves, "Yeah? Prove it..." rather than, "Oh, goody...a hardworking, extra-mile kinda guy!" Another reason *not* to include difficult-to-prove statements about your character is that *most other job searchers are attempting to do the same thing* (ineffectively, I'll add!). So instead of *saying* you're an awesome person, *show* it in your cover letter by including a few powerful pieces of evidence.

Why It's Worth Doing

After observing the results of thousands of job hunters, I've discovered that most people devote the majority of their time to creating cover letters and resumes. Although writing effective resumes and cover letters is an important activity, it certainly doesn't deserve to receive the majority of your job search effort.

Within my career counseling circle of professionals, we refer to spending an excessive amount of time and effort on job search documents as "Polishing the brochure," meaning that instead of using your resumes and cover letters as useful tools to move you forward, you get caught in the trap of trying to make them perfect—and miss out on many valuable opportunities as a result.

By using a proven approach to creating cover letters, requiring you to invest a minimum of time and effort, you will be able to achieve more of what you want in your job search and career.

Career Champ Profile: Julia

Julia was eager to land a new position in event coordination, but was discouraged at the amount of time it took her to create an effective cover letter. "I want the hiring manager to *know* that I'm dedicated and quality minded, but I'm having a terrible time communicating that in my letters!" I encouraged Julia to not attempt to describe her best personal qualities in a cover letter (a daunting task for even the most gifted writers) and instead, to use my tried-and-true formula. Figure 6.1 is Julia's letter, and she was thrilled with the results.

Julia Jones   *Event Coordinator*

6439 Whitmore Court
Fort Collins, CO 80523
(970) 231-8500, juliajones@hotmail.com

October 12, 2008
Carolyn Scott
Celebrations
1234 Skycloud Way
Loveland, CO 80535

Dear Ms. Scott,

Our mutual acquaintance, Forrest O'Neill, has talked to me about you and your organization, and encouraged me to apply to your current opening for an **Event Coordinator.** Your business's outstanding reputation for delivering quality, memorable events is of high interest to me, and is a good match for my approach to event management. Following are highlights of my background as they may pertain to your current or future needs:

➢ Regarding your requirement for an experienced professional, **I have successfully planned and executed events for 100+, with outstanding results.** Clients include Spanish/English speakers with specific cultural considerations and needs. Feedback from event guests has been excellent.

➢ Your advertisement also mentioned, "Formal event management training preferred." **My training includes successful completion of a comprehensive 14-course Bridal Consulting program,** covering topics ranging from etiquette to planning to catering. Received 95 percent overall GPA. (Course listing available on request.)

➢ Additionally, my experience includes numerous customer service positions, addressing your desire for proven strengths in this area. **I have received numerous letters of appreciation from satisfied clients, as well as consistently high ratings in this area on my annual performance evaluations.**

Further details about my background are included on the enclosed resume. I would welcome the opportunity to talk with you about how my experience and qualifications may benefit your organization. In the next few days, I will follow up with to you confirm receipt of this information and to determine a logical next step.

Thank you in advance for your consideration of my qualifications and interest.

Sincerely,

Julia Jones

P.S. I am fluent in both English and Spanish, which enables me to successfully communicate with clientele and guests from diverse backgrounds.

Figure 6.1: Julia's letter.

Core Courage Concept

Writing effective letters to support your job search can seem overwhelming, especially to Career Cowards. How do you communicate your best qualities in a concise, compelling letter, while also motivating the decision maker to call you for an interview? Yikes—what pressure! Rather than make yourself crazy attempting to achieve this near-impossible feat, it makes sense to stick with a proven approach, devoting your time to filling in the details that are relevant to you. Will it feel strange, trying a different approach? Probably…but give it a go, and see how it works for you.

Confidence Checklist

- ☐ Set up your letter professionally.
- ☐ Begin your letter with a to-the-point first paragraph.
- ☐ List three bullets highlighting the most important aspects of your background.
- ☐ Conclude your letter with proposed next steps.
- ☐ P.S…finish strong!

Chapter 7

Use These Secrets to Improve Your Job Application Results

Your job search toolbox is stocked and ready to use; it's filled with a well-researched target list, a dynamite resume, and a customized cover letter. Now it's time to get results for all of your hard work! In this chapter, you'll learn valuable, easy-sneezy steps to significantly increase the number of calls for interviews you receive as you apply to advertised openings.

Risk It or Run From It?

- **Risk Rating:** No or very little risk (depends on how many of these tips you choose to use).

- **Payoff Potential:** Fantabulous! These simple little steps can make a huge difference in the number of interviews your applications generate.

- **Time to Complete:** If you used all of the tips in this chapter for each application, it would take you about 20 minutes per job application package.

- **Bailout Strategy:** These suggestions are extras—bonus activities that will go a long way toward setting you apart from the competition. Technically, you don't need to do them

(continued)

(continued)

> at all. (But if you want to generate more interviews for great positions, they're a good idea!)
>
> - **The "20 Percent Extra" Edge:** The vast majority of job searchers put a minimal amount of effort into their job application efforts. By investing just a little more time, you can help your resume stand above the rest.
>
> - **"Go For It!" Bonus Activity:** Create an "extra steps" checklist to follow when preparing job applications to make sure that you take advantage of all the opportunities to get noticed.

How to Implement Simple Steps to Greatly Improve Your Application Results

Recently, I bought a pair of shoes from an online retailer. Typically ordering shoes is a traumatic experience for me. I have big feet (I won't embarrass myself by going into details), and finding shoes is usually frustrating, often resulting in my settling for something I really don't like. So ordering online seemed like a long shot, but I decided to give it a try, halfway expecting the experience to be a dismal failure.

But this shopping experience turned out to be a "Wow!" experience! For starters, the retailer's Web page was attractive and easy to navigate, with fun, encouraging shopper messages like, "Your order is almost complete. Just one more step!" And when I received my new shoes (I *loved* them, by the way, and they fit great), I was delighted to discover a handwritten note in the box from the service representative saying, "Hope you love these!" Bottom line, I was completely jazzed by this shoe-buying adventure.

Looking back, the little extra steps the shoe company took weren't that big of a deal—making sure that its Web site was well organized, providing me encouraging messages as I placed my order, and including a small handwritten note. But from my perspective, they made a *huge* difference…one that has motivated me to shop with that company a number of times since.

With just a little extra time and effort, you can create the same kind of "Wow!" experience for potential employers, as you prepare and submit your applications, and generate more interviews as a result.

Identify the Important Decision Makers

You know how your heart jumps when you receive a neatly pre-pared envelope displaying your name spelled correctly…and how your heart sinks when you get sent a letter with "Resident" on the label, or your name misspelled? Hiring managers and resume screeners experience the same excitement and disappointment as they sort through the many applications they receive. So it's worth it to invest some time and effort in finding and correctly spelling the resume screeners' names. Sure, you can always default to the standard (and pretty boring) "Dear Sir or Madam," but I recommend that you use one or more of these methods:

- **Use a search engine to research contact names.** In many cases you can locate the names of department managers and hiring coordinators within companies by simply entering the correct keywords into a search engine, such as Google. For instance, you could enter, "Vice President Marketing Great Balls of Fire, Inc." to see if his or her name is listed anywhere on the Internet. Or try, "Human Resources Great Balls of Fire, Inc." to locate a representative within the personnel department. As you uncover names using this method, be sure to verify that the contacts are still currently in those positions by executing this next step…

- **Call the company directly and ask for the names of the key contacts.** Simply phone the business and say, "I would like to verify the name and spelling of the head of the widgets depart-ment." If you have a name that you've researched on the Internet, you can also say, "Is it still Rachel Jones?"

- If you're asked, "Why do you need this information?" answer with, "I'm responding to your job ad and I want to make sure I spell her name correctly." If this step makes you nervous, enlist the help of a friend or job search supporter to do it for you. And if the ad clearly states, "No calls," don't call!

Panic Point! "Yikes, call the company directly! Won't they get mad?" I know, I know...the thought of calling a potential employer directly to gather info about contacts can seem pretty scary. Many Career Cowards fear that the hiring manager might actually pick up the phone (she might), and that for some reason she won't like the sound of your voice. Other Career Cowards worry that a mean receptionist will tell them to go jump in a lake. So yes, it can seem scary to call. Yet consider this: Throughout my many years of helping clients find the contact names they need—either by assisting them with what to say or making the calls for them—the person at the company who answers the phone ends up giving us the information we want *75 percent of the time*. Those are pretty good odds! And if they don't give us the name, they don't yell at us. Instead, they say something like, "I'm not allowed to give out that information." In the thousands of times we've used this technique, I have *never* encountered or heard of a scary hiring manager or receptionist responding with, "Get lost, you loser!" So go ahead...give it a try! Chances are you'll wind up with the names you want.

Mention Any Mutual Acquaintances

Staying on the topic of names, be sure to mention any mutual acquaintances in your cover letter. For example, let's say that Lance Mercer, a vendor you know from Spiffy Products, told you about an opening at Great Balls of Fire, Inc., and encouraged you to apply. He knows the VP of Marketing at Great Balls of Fire, Inc., personally.

In the first paragraph of your cover letter, you could write this:

> Lance Mercer, a mutual acquaintance, told me about the opening within your company and encouraged me to apply.

Mentioning Lance's name will give you instant credibility, and again, will help you stand out from the other applicants. If you don't have a mutual acquaintance, consider sending a message to people in your network to see whether anyone has a connection to the hiring manager or human resources representative.

Include Keywords in Your Resume and Cover Letter

In chapters 5 and 6, I detailed the importance of including keywords in your resumes and cover letters, but it's worth emphasizing again. By including keywords—including the title for the position—in your cover letter and resume, you significantly increase your chances of being selected for an interview, especially if the business uses keyword filter technology in its sorting process. And if your application is being reviewed by a human being, that individual will respond positively to seeing the right words in your materials.

Research the Company's Priorities

Similar to including keywords from a job description in your materials, it's also a good idea to incorporate phrases that relate to the company's priorities. Spend a few minutes researching the hiring company on the Internet. Be on the lookout for key phrases that describe the company's mission, culture, and products. Then find ways to work that verbiage into your materials. For instance, you could write something like this:

> Your company's focus on creating and maintaining sustainable operations is admirable, and is in line with my own values. When I worked at Company X, I organized and launched the first sustainability review task force...

Create a Flawless Application

When you apply to an advertised opening, some businesses will require you to complete a formal application, by filling out either an online or hardcopy document. To improve your chances of being selected for an interview, follow these formal application guidelines:

- **Complete the application in full.** To you, some of the questions asked on an application might seem silly, redundant, or prying. However, if a company uses an application in its hiring process, you need to take it seriously, and complete it fully and without errors.

- **Create a cheat sheet.** If you have trouble remembering details, fill in a sample job application (print one off of a company's Web page or pick one up from a potential employer), and keep this cheat sheet on hand. Resist the urge to guess on details—those errors could come back to haunt you.

- **Don't omit information about pay.** Instead, include a range when providing information about former salary (list starting and ending—and factor in bonuses and benefits if you want to bump it up a little), and write "open" or "negotiable" when responding to questions about desired compensation.

Panic Point! Worried about including salary information when a company asks for it? You're right...it can feel like an employer is invading your privacy by asking something so personal. "What right do they have to ask?" you might wonder. Keep in mind that for larger employers especially, their goal is to standardize and streamline their hiring processes to deal with the thousands of job applications they receive each year. Gathering information about your pay is one way those companies can streamline their sorting processes to determine whether you're a fit for a position that interests you. For this reason, it's important to include *something* when you're asked for this information on an application—"Will discuss in interview," or a low-high range detailing the upper and lower ends of your former compensation. Even though it might make you squirm a little, don't leave these blocks on an application blank—otherwise, you could be booted from consideration.

Keep in mind that employers can check back only five to seven years into your work history. If you don't want to list a former employer from further back into your employment, you don't need to.

Submit Your Application on Quality Paper, in a Larger Envelope

If you choose to submit a hardcopy version of your application (and I strongly recommend that you do—I'll give more details on this in chapter 8), print your materials on resume-quality paper. White or cream-colored is best, and be sure to sign your cover letters! (On average, 25 percent of job searchers forget this important step.)

When your resume and cover letters are ready, mail them in a 9 × 12 manila envelope. This will allow your materials to arrive flat, making them easier for the hiring coordinator to handle and photocopy. A larger envelope is also more noticeable within a large stack of envelopes. But don't bother sending materials in overnight packaging (unless you must to meet a submission deadline). Doing so can make you appear wasteful, as well as draw attention to what could be perceived as poor time management on your part.

Send Applications to Both the Hiring Manager and the HR Rep

This is an easy-to-execute activity that generates great results. As you prepare an application in response to a job opening, plan to submit materials to both the hiring manager (the person you would end up reporting to) as well as to the human resources representative. Most job hunters send their materials *only* to human resources. Yet keep in mind the HR reps are *not* the ultimate decision makers—that power lies with your future boss! So send her a package, too.

Keep Records of What You've Submitted

Down the line, when the hiring company calls to schedule an interview, you might need to refer to the materials you submitted. For this reason, it's a good idea to print and file a copy of each of your applications, cover letters, and resumes. In chapter 10, I'll tell you more about how to file and track these materials.

Why It's Worth Doing

The vast majority of job searchers put very little time into customizing their resumes and cover letters. By putting in just a little extra effort on each application—researching appropriate contact names, finding out and including a sentence or two about the company, sending a set of materials to both the HR rep and the hiring manager—you can quickly and easily rise above the crowd of other applicants, and greatly increase your chances of being called in for an interview. A few extra minutes invested when you prepare your applications can shorten your job search and open doors to many more attractive job opportunities!

Career Champ Profile: Meredith

I could see that Meredith was physically shaking, sitting in her chair in my office. "I'm *really* nervous," she admitted. "I know that it's a good idea to try to get the name of the hiring manager, so that I can send him an application, too. But the idea of calling the company to get his name terrifies me!"

Over the last few weeks, Meredith and I had been working on ways to improve her job applications and boost her rate of interviews. One suggestion I'd given her was to find out the name of the hiring manager and to send that person a copy of her application materials, as well as send a set to the HR representative. She agreed that the idea was a good one, but as of yet, she'd been too scared to actually contact companies to obtain this information.

"Let's see what we can find on the Internet, first," I suggested, and I turned my monitor so that we could both see the screen. "This opening is for a Manufacturing Engineer at Quality Inc, right? So you'd most likely report to the Director of Manufacturing. Let's see what's out there." I went to Google and typed in, "Director of Manufacturing Quality Inc." and hit "Search." Several citations popped up on my screen, including the company's Web page. We visited there first, looking for names of team members somewhere on the site, but none were provided.

We went back to Google and clicked on a few of the other links our search had generated. One of the citations pulled up a press release about a product Quality, Inc., had launched the preceding year. The Director of Manufacturing, Duane Johnston, was mentioned in the article. "There's a clue!" I said excitedly. "So now you just need to call the company and verify that Duane is still the manufacturing director. Want to give it a try?" Meredith pulled out her script and nodded slightly, agreeing to make the call, but still looking pretty nervous about it. "I'll step out of my office so that you can have some privacy. Good luck!"

Two minutes later, Meredith bounded out of my office, a huge smile on her face. "I did it! I did it! I did it!" she exclaimed. "Yes, Duane is still the Director of Manufacturing there, so I'll send him an application packet, too. I'm so proud of myself!"

Core Courage Concept

When it comes to preparing job applications, the easiest route is to slap a "Dear Sir or Madam" on your cover letter and submit it along with your standard resume. For Career Cowards, this can seem "safe" as well as easy. Yet this approach doesn't usually generate very good results. By investing a little more effort—and taking steps that might make your heart pound, such as calling the potential employer to obtain the hiring manager's name—you can quickly set yourself apart from the competition and greatly improve your job search results. Will it make you squirm a little? Probably. But this is an ideal time to build your courage muscles!

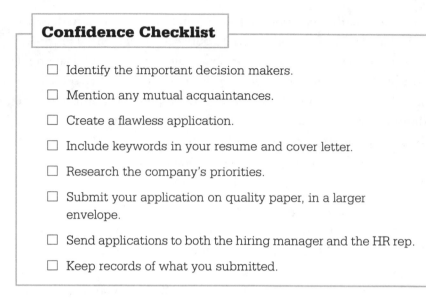

Confidence Checklist

☐ Identify the important decision makers.

☐ Mention any mutual acquaintances.

☐ Create a flawless application.

☐ Include keywords in your resume and cover letter.

☐ Research the company's priorities.

☐ Submit your application on quality paper, in a larger envelope.

☐ Send applications to both the hiring manager and the HR rep.

☐ Keep records of what you submitted.

Chapter 8

Follow Up to Land More Interviews

Congrats! You're putting in the extra time and effort to truly help your application materials stand out from among the competition. Your application form is complete and flawless. Maintain your positive momentum by following through on the applications you submit, using the effective tips provided in this chapter.

Risk It or Run From It?

- **Risk Rating:** Minimal to mid-range, related to the suggestions you choose to use.

- **Payoff Potential:** Very, very high. Only a miniscule percentage of job searchers go to the effort to follow through on their applications. Doing so will greatly increase your chances for success.

- **Time to Complete:** A few minutes per application.

- **Bailout Strategy:** Just like the suggestions provided in the preceding chapter, these are extra steps that, in theory, you don't need to do. However, if you're looking for easy ways to significantly increase your job search results, give them a try.

(continued)

(continued)

> * **The "20 Percent Extra" Edge:** Based on my observations, fewer than 10 percent of job searchers follow up on the job applications they've submitted. By doing so, you instantly launch yourself into cream-of-the-crop status.
>
> * **"Go For It!" Bonus Activity:** As you follow up on resumes you've submitted, keep track of the percentage of positive results you get. It will motivate you to keep on plugging!

How to Go the Extra Mile to Boost Your Application Successes

At my house, we have a saying: "Be sure to FTJ!" This motto evolved over the years as we've attempted to teach our kids (and okay, I'll admit that the adults need to hear it sometimes, too) to Finish the Job. You and I both know how tempting it is to want to wrap things up as soon as possible, even though there are a few loose ends still waiting to be tied. Following are some suggestions for improving your application results with some proven FTJ techniques.

Send a Second Submission

This tip is one of my all-time favorites: After you've applied to a potential employer, print a second, identical hardcopy version of your materials (cover letter, resume, and application form if the company requires it). Then, somewhere on your cover letter (the top-right corner is a good place) handwrite this message:

> *Second submission–I'm very interested*

Send the materials with your handwritten note via snail mail to the employer. This simple step can significantly improve your chances of receiving a call for an interview. Why? Many human resources representatives have told me, although they request online submissions, they miss the tangible feel of a thoughtfully produced resume and cover letter printed on quality paper. *When you send a hardcopy application, you set yourself apart from the crowd of electronic applicants.*

Also, by submitting your materials more than one time (electronic and hardcopy, or two hardcopy versions), you increase your chances of being noticed. Your handwritten, "Second submission–I'm very interested" message shows that you're truly interested.

Make Follow-Up Calls

After you've sent two copies of your materials—the original and the second-submission versions—make a note on your calendar to call in three business days to follow up. This will allow you to

- Confirm that your materials were received successfully (sometimes they don't make it to the intended recipient, especially if they were submitted electronically).

- Find out what will happen next in the hiring process.

- Make a personal connection with a screener.

Use these steps to follow up effectively:

1. Follow up three business days after you've sent your second submission.

2. Call the company and ask to speak to the hiring manager in charge of the position (whose name you should already know).

3. Communicate the following information, either directly to the individual, or on his or her voice mail:

   "Hello, this is YOUR NAME. I am calling regarding the POSITION TITLE currently open within your organization. I want to confirm that my application materials were received successfully, and also to find out more about what will happen next in your hiring process."

4. Include your phone number if you're leaving a voice-mail message, and mention that you sent a second set of materials, with a handwritten "Second Submission" message.

Panic Point! Does the thought of following up on your application terrify you? Would you rather have your fingernails pulled out one by one? If so, you're not alone! Most Career Cowards *dread* the thought of making a follow-up call after submitting an application, fearing that they'll be verbally rejected on the spot, as in, "Don't bug me! I'm not hiring you!" However, in my many years of assisting thousands of job searchers, this kind of humiliating rejection has never happened. Still, I know the fear is real. So to help you sidestep this worry, I recommend that you make your phone call either before 7 a.m., or after 7 p.m., when you're most likely to reach voice mail rather than a real person, and simply leave a message.

If you want to take your follow-up even further, call one week later, leaving a message like this:

> *Hello, NAME OF HIRING MANAGER. It's YOUR NAME, calling back to say that I'm still very interested in your opening, and I'm hopeful that I'll be called in for an interview. If it turns out that I'm not chosen, I wish you the best in finding the right person for the job, and please keep me in mind for future opportunities.*

This leaves the hiring manager with a good impression of your interest and professionalism, as well as gives you peace of mind to know that you did a thorough job of following through.

Recontact Interesting Companies Six Months Later

Let's say that in January, you applied to the opening at Great Balls of Fire, Inc., a manufacturer of fireworks, and you love the idea of working for a business that makes things explode! You also sent a second submission, but didn't get called in for an interview. You're bummed, because it looked like a great position. Instead of writing off this opportunity forever, make a note on your calendar to recontact the hiring manager in June. Why? Because on average, *40 percent of individuals hired for a position don't work out within the first six months.* Either they've already quit because the job wasn't right for them…or they've been fired because they weren't succeeding…or (and this is the most common scenario) they're still working at the job, but the boss isn't happy with their performance.

By following up six months later, you might connect with the hiring manager at the exact time that she's ready to make a change. Either call the hiring manager directly and let her know that you're still interested, or resubmit the materials (yes, a *third* submission!) that you sent originally, this time with a handwritten message stating that you are still very interested.

Use One Potential Employer to Lead You to Others

For example, let's imagine that the idea of working for Great Balls of Fire, Inc., really jazzes you. You love the idea of working for a fireworks manufacturer! So as soon as you've completed your first and second submissions to that company, take a few minutes to research other fireworks manufacturers, and then prepare materials (you can even reuse much of what you sent to the first company) to send to them, *even if they don't have any advertised positions available.*

This falls within the category of approaching companies directly (chapter 9 provides more details on this activity) and is extremely effective. Why? Because when a position opens at one company within an industry, it very often affects positions at other companies, as specialists shuffle from one company to another within that industry. Submitting a cover letter and resume directly to those other employers improves your chances of locating an opening before it ever gets advertised. Then, instead of competing against 100 other applicants, you would be the only one!

Why It's Worth Doing

I don't *really* need to tell you why it's so important to follow through on the applications you submit. What might be worth a little discussion, however, is why it's important for you to push through your fear of doing it.

Think about a time when you applied to a position that seemed very interesting to you, but that you weren't interviewed for. Got one in mind? Good. Now take a rough guess at how much time you've thought about that opportunity since you applied to it. Based on many conversations with clients, I would estimate that job searchers think about jobs they were highly interested in, but didn't get called about, an average of five minutes a day, often over a period of at least two months. Conservatively, that's *five hours!* Multiply those five hours by all the other job opportunities for which you've applied.

Why do you do it? Because, according to your brain, the opportunity is still open—it's a loose end that your mind needs to track. Yet instinctively you know that ruminating over unfulfilled job opportunities is a *terrible* waste of your time and energy.

So let's imagine a different scenario. Let's say, for instance, that you applied to a position that looked interesting, and instead of just cogitating on it day after day, you decide to do some follow-up. You print off and submit a hardcopy "second submission" package, an activity that takes you five minutes to complete. Three days later, you make a follow-up call (you call at 8 p.m. to reduce the chances of someone actually answering, but hey, you're calling!) and leave a message using the script provided in this chapter. This step took you three minutes. As a final follow-through activity, you leave a second message a week later, investing another three minutes of your time.

In total, you've invested 11 minutes of your time on highly productive follow-up activities and significantly improved your chances of being called in for an interview. But even more important, *you've given your brain a reason to stop pondering about the opportunity over and over day after day*, because it knows you've done your part to wrap things up, and you can let it go. *That's* why it's worth doing!

Career Champ Profile: Amory

For almost a year, Amory had been inching along in his job search, sending out resumes to job postings he found on the Internet that looked interesting. But his results were poor, and with each passing week, he was getting more and more frustrated. I asked him to tell me about his job search process, as well as the results he was getting.

"Well, I find ads on the Internet and send them a resume and cover letter. I hear back from companies less than 10 percent of the time, so I feel as if I'm doing something wrong," he responded. Analyzing his process a little further, I learned that Amory had no system in place for following up on the applications he submitted.

"Let's try this," I suggested. "For the next month, every time you submit an electronic application, send a hardcopy of your materials to the company as well. Just print out the same cover letter and resume you submitted the first time, on resume-quality paper. Handwrite, 'Second submission, I'm very interested,' somewhere on the cover letter…oh and be sure to sign the letter, too. Sometimes people forget to do that. Snail mail those hardcopy materials the same day you send the electronic application."

Amory looked at me as if I needed to have my head examined. "That's it? Just that little extra step?" he asked. I told him there were many other steps we could take to improve the results he was getting, but that this was a good place to begin. "We can add in more in the next few weeks. But for now, start with this one."

A week later, when I picked up my voice-mail messages, there was one from Amory. He was laughing. "I can't believe this," he began, "but that 'second submission' thing really worked! Yesterday I received a call from the VP of R&D at a company I applied to last week. He said he was driving home after work, but that he wanted to give me a call because he'd received my package, and that I seemed really interested. He said he liked my persistence! So he interviewed me for 15 minutes and is making arrangements to fly me out for a formal interview next week. I can't believe it!"

Over the next two months, Amory sent out more than 30 hardcopy packages of his application materials, with "second submission" messages handwritten on the cover letters, and his rate of calls for interviews increased by 50 percent! Within three months, he'd landed a great job with one of his target companies.

Core Courage Concept

Follow up on applications you've submitted? Eek! For Career Cowards especially, this is a *terrifying* activity to consider doing. What if you get rejected? What if the hiring manager yells at you? What if some other horrible result happens? The "what ifs" surrounding follow-through can be endless and overwhelming. But instead of writing off the idea entirely, challenge yourself to experiment with small steps. Send a "second submission," or practice making a follow-up phone call. Like a muscle that rarely gets used, you might be pleasantly surprised to discover that once you begin, you can build your strength much easier, and less painfully, than you feared.

Confidence Checklist

- ☐ Send a second submission.
- ☐ Make follow-up calls.
- ☐ Recontact interesting companies six months later.
- ☐ Use one potential employer to lead you to others.

Chapter 9

Connect with Even More Employers

W e've discussed the "hidden job market"—that mysterious pool of openings that aren't obvious to the typical job searcher. In this chapter, you're going to find out how to dip into that resource and significantly expand the number of job opportunities available to you. Making use of this single job hunting method can quickly transform your job search from so-so to Go, Go! So read on to find out how to put this exciting, powerful job search tool to work for you.

Risk It or Run From It?

- **Risk Rating:** Most likely, this step will seem a little scary. It's true, there is a bit of risk involved...but the payoff is definitely worth it. So keep reading and take it one tiny step at a time.

- **Payoff Potential:** So huge! Implement the simple steps in this chapter and your job search results can skyrocket.

- **Time to Complete:** Preparing your materials, sending them, and following up will take about 15 minutes per company.

- **Bailout Strategy:** Ask someone else to do the prep work and distribute your materials for you. Or just experiment with

(continued)

(continued)

these techniques to see how they work for you. Or skip it altogether (but I really don't want you to).

- **The "20 Percent Extra" Edge:** Most job searchers never even think of connecting with employers unless they have a job ad posted. By being proactive and putting your materials in front of the hiring manager, you increase your chances for being at the right place at the right time.

- **"Go For It!" Bonus Activity:** When you identify a company that looks especially interesting to you, contact a few colleagues in your industry and ask whether they have any contacts within the organization, and whether you can mention their names when you contact a company representative.

How to Show Future Employers What You Have to Offer

You *know* you have great skills, experience, and talents to offer to an employer. But do employers know about you? Chances are, they don't. In fact, it's very likely that the majority of companies who would want to hire you don't even know you exist. It's sad but true. However, you can easily turn this situation around by following the steps described in this chapter.

Review Your Target List

Remember the target list you created in chapter 4? It's really going to come in handy now. Pull it out and look over the list of 20+ company names you've researched. These are employers who can potentially benefit from what you have to offer. If your list needs more work (or if you haven't created it yet), refer to chapter 4 for suggestions on how to identify companies that are a good fit for you.

Prepare Powerful Letters of Introduction

In chapter 6, we discussed how to put together an easy-to-create, effective cover letter. Building on this same successful format, you'll now learn how to create a letter that will allow you to effectively introduce yourself to potential employers. Figure 9.1 is an example of the same cover letter shown in chapter 6, with some small changes.

J. J.   *Event Coordinator*

Northern Colorado
(970) 231-8500, jjnortherncolorado@hotmail.com
October 12, 2008

Reid Wilkins
Events Extraordinaire
3225 Parkway Place
Denver, CO 80245

Dear Mr. Wilkins,

After researching your company and learning about its impressive reputation in the Denver events management community, I am writing to introduce myself as a potential **Event Coordinator** resource for your organization. Following are highlights of my background as they might pertain to your current or future needs:

> ➤ **I have successfully planned and executed events for 100+, with outstanding results.** Clients include Spanish/English speakers with specific cultural considerations and needs. Feedback from event guests has been excellent.
> ➤ **My training includes successful completion of a comprehensive 14-course Bridal Consulting program,** covering topics ranging from etiquette to planning to catering. Received 95 percent overall GPA. (Course listing available on request.)
> ➤ Additionally, my experience includes numerous customer service positions, addressing your desire for proven strengths in this area. **I have received numerous letters of appreciation from satisfied clients, as well as consistently high ratings in this area on my annual performance evaluations.**

After Further details about my background are included on the enclosed resume. In respect to the relationship I have with my current employer, I have listed only my initials in this correspondence. However, I would welcome the opportunity to introduce myself fully, and to talk with you about how my experience and qualifications might benefit your organization, either by phone or an in-person conversation. In the next few days, I will follow up with you to confirm receipt of this information and to determine a logical next step.

Thank you in advance for your consideration of my qualifications and interest.

Sincerely,

J. J.

P.S. I am fluent in both English and Spanish, which enables me to successfully communicate with clientele and guests from diverse backgrounds.

Figure 9.1: A cover letter altered to introduce yourself to an employer.

As you can see, the letters are practically identical, with only a few differences:

- **Name and address information:** This information will be customized to include specifics pertaining to a target employer on your list. Refer to your target list for these details.

- **Opening paragraph:** Instead of referring to an advertised job, as you would if there were an actual opening available, you are instead introducing yourself as a *potential* resource.

- **Bullet statements:** Instead of listing a specific requirement (again, because you aren't responding to a job ad), you'll need to keep your bullet statements more generic. As you can see, we simply removed the opening statement in each bullet to make it more general. Easy!

Panic Point! Are you just now realizing that I'm suggesting that you mail your resume and letter of introduction to employers who *aren't even advertising for employees*? And does the idea of this make you uncomfortable? Well, you're not alone in this concern. Most job searchers I've counseled are *very* reluctant to take this step. They worry about things like, "What if the employer isn't even interested? What if she's perfectly happy with the employees she has now? What if she thinks I'm an idiot for mailing her my resume? What if she immediately dumps my materials in the trash?" Yes, there are a lot of "what-ifs" and unknowns when it comes to approaching companies directly. Yet consider this: Many employers would be thrilled to consider you as a resource, *if they only knew you were available!* Sure, you'll experience some rejection with this activity. But you also experience rejection when you apply to advertised positions—so what's the difference? Even more important to consider is the fact that *many* employers are in desperate need of someone with your experience and talents. So read on, and chances are you'll feel more comfortable with this idea as you learn more about it.

Create "Consider Me!" Packages

You're really on your way now. You have a list of target employers who would be interested in learning about what you have to offer. You've begun to create your direct approach letters. Now all you need to do is mail these letters to potential employers along with a resume.

Panic Point! Does it make you uncomfortable broadcasting your name far and wide to potential hiring managers, in fear that your current employer will find out that you're job hunting? This is a valid concern. To minimize any potential problems, consider preparing resumes and direct approach letters that will allow you to maintain your confidentiality. Create a header on your cover letter and resume that includes only your initials, mention the region where you live (rather than your specific address), and list a cell phone number and e-mail address that do not reveal your identity. Also, include a line explaining your reason for maintaining your confidentiality in your cover letter, as we've done in figure 9.1.

Also, check out the recommendations offered in chapter 5 for improving your success rates, such as mailing hardcopies of your direct-approach packages in 9 × 12 envelopes, so that your materials arrive unfolded and in pristine condition.

Stagger the Mailing of Your Packages Over Time

You've created a list of 20 or more target companies. You could, in theory, mail 20 or more direct-approach packages all at once. However, I recommend that you start more slowly, mailing just a few each day. Why? Because if you mail too many at one time, it could be difficult for you to follow up on all of them in a timely manner. We'll discuss effective, doable ways to follow up in chapter 11. But for now, choose a pace that feels reasonable to you and begin mailing out your materials.

Why It's Worth Doing

Imagine that you are a successful business owner. You run Cool-o Company, and your work is meaningful and interesting. For the most part, you love what you do. The only little fly in the ointment is that occasionally, you end up with a member on your team who isn't working out.

In fact, you have that problem right now. Three months ago you hired a new office manager, Lena, to replace Jill, who had been your office manager for two years. Jill had been great in her job, but she moved out of state, so you went through a hiring process to replace her.

The hiring process was a bit of a nightmare. You advertised on www.monster.com and ran an ad in the local paper, and were flooded with applications—more than 100! You spent hours going through those resumes, but in the end, only eight applicants really looked as if they'd fit the job. You called in five of them for interviews, hoping to find a new "Jill" among the bunch.

It didn't work out that way. Of the five candidates you interviewed, only two seemed acceptable, but neither of them really impressed you. Still, Jill had already been gone for two weeks, and you were in desperate need of an office manager, so you offered the job to Lena.

That was three months ago. Since then, it has become more and more obvious that Lena isn't working out, and you've started to think about firing her. But the idea of running another ad, interviewing people again, and still not knowing whether you'll find someone better has held you back.

Just then, the daily mail arrives. Flipping through the stack, you notice an envelope hand-addressed to you. You pull it out and open it. It's a letter and resume from Charlotte, and she's writing to introduce herself as a potential office manager for Cool-o Company. "Hmmm," you think. "Could this be the answer I've been looking for?" You carefully read through her resume and are impressed with what she has to offer. But just then Lena sticks her head into your office. "You have a call from one of our important customers." Distracted, you set Charlotte's letter in a stack of papers and forget about it for a while.

A few days later, you arrive at your office and check your voice mail. There's a message from Charlotte! She says, "I'm following up on a resume I sent you a few days ago. I'd like to set a time to meet you briefly. Would Thursday morning or Friday afternoon this week work for you? My phone number is...."

Wow, this Charlotte chick really seems to have her act together! You phone her to set up a meeting. What could it hurt? She might be just what you're looking for—without the hassle of needing to go through another complicated hiring process.

Decision makers—especially wise, growth-oriented ones (the kinds you want to work for) are *always* on the lookout for quality talent. So if you, like Charlotte, were to present yourself directly to some of those decision makers, you would very likely discover that those managers and business owners would be open to talking with you. Yet, get this: *Less than 10 percent of job searchers ever go to the effort of approaching potential employers directly.* As a result, multitudes of job opportunities exist in the world of work, but job searchers aren't going after them!

So, yes, yes, yes, approaching companies directly is worth it! Just try a few and see. I predict that you'll be *very* pleased with the results.

Career Champ Profile: Kiley

"Here's what I've researched so far for my target list," Kiley said, showing me a typed page of company names. "There are some very interesting companies around here," she continued. "I had no idea! It was pretty exciting thinking about all of the possibilities once I began looking into these potential employers more closely."

"Excellent!" I responded. "How are you feeling about connecting with them by mailing some direct-approach packages?" Kiley admitted the idea made her a little nervous. "I realize that when I contact these companies, most of them won't be hiring. But I do feel confident that my background in information systems would be a huge asset to the right business, if they are on the lookout for someone good. So, why not send out some letters and resumes, right? What could it hurt?"

Kiley and I looked over her letter of introduction and resume. To avoid the awkward situation of her current employer finding out about her job search, Kiley had chosen to list just her initials, K.S., her region, Northern Colorado, and nonidentifying e-mail and cell phone numbers. "I prepared four packages I plan to mail this week, one for each day," she told me, showing me the printouts of her letters and resumes. "I'll mail the first one on Monday, and begin my follow-up calls and e-mails on Wednesday. I'm nervous, but I'm also motivated to find work that's right for me. Wish me luck!"

About a week later, Kiley sent me an e-mail update: "The first two places I contacted didn't want to meet with me. But the third place I called set an appointment right away! Turns out that the company is currently expanding the IT department and they've been looking for someone with my background. I'll keep you posted!"

Core Courage Concept

Out of all of the job search suggestions I present in this book, I know that the idea of approaching companies directly is one of the most frightening for Career Cowards to try. But just like other intimidating things you've attempted in your life—riding a two-wheeler bike, or asking someone out on a date, for instance—trying new things (although scary) can take you to new, wonderful places you've only dreamed of.

Confidence Checklist

☐ Review your target list.

☐ Prepare powerful letters of introduction.

☐ Create "consider me!" packages.

☐ Stagger the mailing of your packages over time.

Chapter 10

Take a Breather and Get Organized for Success

By now you might be feeling a little overwhelmed with how to manage the many job search tools you've developed—your company target list, resume, cover letters, direct approach letters, and so on. In this chapter, I'll walk you through a fun, easy way to put these resources in order, using an organization system that will help you feel in control and position you to succeed in your search.

Risk It or Run From It?

- **Risk Rating:** Low, low, low—like organizing your closet.

- **Payoff Potential:** Terrific! Getting your job search materials in order will feel great and allow you to more easily succeed with the next steps in your search.

- **Time to Complete:** About an hour.

- **Bailout Strategy:** Well, you don't have to use the organization system I'm suggesting. You might already have one you like. In that case, skip this chapter. Or you could just stay disorganized and hope that things don't fall through the cracks.

(continued)

(continued)

- **The "20 Percent Extra" Edge:** Being organized saves time, builds confidence, and gives you more energy to move forward in your search.

- **"Go For It!" Bonus Activity:** Take a trip to an office-supply store to scope out other helpful organization materials. The right tools can be both motivating and time-saving.

How to Set Yourself Up for Smooth Searching

You've already done so much work toward setting yourself up for a results-producing job hunt. Your target list, resumes, and letters give you a strong foundation. Now we'll invest just a little time in getting all of these materials in order so that you can use them easily and successfully.

Gather Your Target List and Organization Supplies

The steps outlined in this chapter will help you create a simple, elegant method for organizing and tracking your job search activities. To set up this system, you'll need the following supplies:

- Your list of 20–100 target employers

- A 1½-inch to 2-inch three-ring binder

- A three-hole punch, or paper that is already three-hole punched

- A set of binder tabs, numbered 1–31 (you need only *one* total set of numbered tabs, *not* one set for each month)

You don't need fancy supplies for this system to work. Use an old binder (we all seem to have one or more kicking around somewhere), buy a pack of three-hole-punched paper for a dollar or two, and make your own binder tabs labeled 1–31 using sticky notes.

Fill In Your Master Company/Contact List

This step is super easy. Use either paper or a computer to create a table that looks like this:

Company/Contact Name	Tab#	Tab#	Tab#	Tab#	Tab#	Tab#	Tab#

Now, in the "Company/Contact Name" column, write in the names of the companies you've researched. It's not essential to list them alphabetically, but you can if you want. Here's an example of what it might look like:

Company/Contact Name	Tab#	Tab#	Tab#	Tab#	Tab#	Tab#	Tab#
A Very Cool Company							
Great Biz, Inc.							
Supreme Corporation							
Matchless Manufacturers							
Unbeatable Corp.							
Ultimate Company							

Create a Company/Contact Info Page for All of Your Target Employers

Next you'll prepare a *separate* company/contact info page for each employer. Again, you can write these up longhand, or type them in a word-processing or spreadsheet file—whichever you prefer. Your employer info pages should look like the following:

Company/Contact Page

Company: _____

Contacts: _____

_____

Address information: _____

_____

_____

Phone/Web/e-mail information: _____

_____

_____

Important product/service information: _____

_____

_____

_____

_____

Action steps/record: _____

_____

_____

_____

_____

_____

Once you've created these pages, fill in as much information as you have at this point, based on the research you've already completed. Here's an example:

Company: A Very Cool Company

Contacts: Serena Lauer, VP Marketing

Address information: 431 Wilson St., Green Hills, CA, 94321

Phone/Web/e-mail information: 444-333-2221, www.averycoolcompany.com, slauer@averycoolcompany.com

Important product/service information: Design and manufacture top-of-the-line products to improve image, efficiency, and lifestyle.

Action steps/record:

Leave the "Action Steps/Record" section blank for now. We'll fill that in next.

Decide on Next Step Action Items for Each Employer

At this point, you should have a stack of company/contact pages, partially filled in. Now you'll want to ask yourself, "What is the next step I want to take with each of these companies?" You'll write this activity in the "Action steps/record" section of each company/contact page. Here are some possible next steps that might be appropriate for each of your target companies:

- Research the company further to learn more about key contacts, products, and services.

- Prepare and mail direct approach letters.

- Follow up on direct approach letters.

- Look at the company's Web site to check out any advertised job openings.

- Prepare an application for an advertised job opening.

- E-mail a few key people in my network to see whether they know anyone at this company.

Panic Point! Are you thinking, "I don't *know* what action I need to take with each of these companies! What should I write down?" Because you haven't used this organization system before, and you're not yet familiar with how it works, you probably feel confused about where this process is going. That's understandable. If the next step that you want to take with each company isn't obvious to you, write, "Research company further," keeping in mind that a little more research about a company would probably be useful. As we move ahead in this job search process, you'll become clearer on other steps you'll want to take with each company. Or, if you feel as if you've researched the company enough, write, "Prepare direct approach letter" as a next-step action item.

Choose "Due By" Dates for Your Action Items

As the final step in setting up your job search organization process, you'll want to decide where to file each of your company/contact pages in your binder. This is the fun part of this system because you'll very quickly begin to see how you can easily and successfully organize and make progress in your job search. The simplest way to determine where you'll file each company/contact page is to decide which day of the month you plan to complete the action item you've listed for that company.

Let's say, for instance, that you've chosen "Prepare and mail direct-approach letter" as your next action step with A Very Cool Company. Looking at your calendar, you decide that you want to prepare and mail this letter on the 29th of this month, so you'll file the company/contact page behind tab #29, which represents the 29th.

Now, to help you keep track of where you've filed this company/contact page in your binder (saving you from flipping through 31 tabs in the future), write "29" in the box next to A Very Cool Company on your master company/contact list. It will look like this:

Company/ Contact Name	Tab#	Tab#	Tab#	Tab#	Tab#	Tab#	Tab#
A Very Cool Company	29						
Great Biz, Inc.							

Repeat this process with each company/contact page, keeping in mind the following tips:

- Set a realistic pace for your job search activities. If you know, for instance, that you'll have time to prepare and mail only two direct-approach packages to target companies each day, file only two company/contact pages behind each date tab.

- File your company/contact pages using a rotating calendar. For example, after you prepare and mail a direct-approach package on April 29, you decide to follow up on May 2 (the next month). So when you complete your action item on the 29th, make a note of the next step in the "Action steps/record" section and file that page behind the #2 tab in your binder (which now represents May 2 because April 2 has already passed).

- Assign a date in the rotating month to complete an action item for *every* one of your target companies. This will keep your job search moving forward successfully. If you need to, keep your action steps small, such as, "Look at company Web page to review new postings." But at all costs, *avoid dumping your company/contact pages into a "To Be Done at Some Random Time in the Future" section.*

- Every time you take some action related to one of your target companies, such as mailing a direct-approach package or applying to an advertised job, print a hardcopy record of the materials you submitted and attach it to the appropriate company/contact page, making it easy for you to access records of your activities.

- Be sure to update the location of each company/contact page on your master list every time you move it, so that you can locate it easily.

- Open up your job search binder to the appropriately numbered tab for that day, and complete the activities you've planned. Repeat this process every day.

Down the line, I'll show you more ways to make use of this powerful job search organization system. But for now, set aside your binder and get ready for the next step in the process.

Why It's Worth Doing

Can you recall a time in your life when you felt truly disorganized? For me, it was when I was about to be married, we were moving into a new home, and boxes and wedding gifts were arriving daily. When my fiancé asked me to pull out some legal records and financial statements, I panicked. Yes, I had them *somewhere* in the house, but I was clueless about where they actually were. At that time in my life, I remember feeling out of control and frustrated.

Now think about a time when you were very organized. For example, I once hired a wardrobe consultant to help me get my clothes and closet in order. For four hours one afternoon, I sorted, tried on, discarded, and reorganized my clothing, shoes, and accessories, following her process. At the end of the session, not only did my closet look great, I felt great about it, knowing that now I could easily locate and pull together outfits that would meet my wardrobe needs. In just a few hours, I went from feeling frustrated to feeling fantastic, simply by putting my closet in order. The anxiety I once felt toward my wardrobe, agonizing over not having the right outfit, evaporated. Rather than, "Oh no, what will I wear?" my attitude shifted to, "I'm ready for any occasion. Bring it on!"

You'll experience the same shift from frustration to motivation as you put your job search materials in order. So when the hiring manager at A Very Cool Company contacts you to say, "I have your resume in front of me, and I have a question about an item you've included. Could we go over that together?" you'll be able to say, "Absolutely! I've got that document right here in front of me...."

Career Champ Profile: Zeke

Zeke was excited. He wanted to land a position as a tour guide for historical sites and cities, and had already researched a list of 30 potential employers. He was jazzed about the potential opportunities available for him, but it was obvious to me that he was feeling overwhelmed. "I'm not sure what to do with all of this stuff," he said, dumping a stack of Internet printouts and handwritten pages in front of me. "This is my company information, but what a mess!"

"Let's get this organized," I suggested, pulling out a binder, a three-hole punch, and a set of tabs, labeled 1–31. "Let's begin by having you find all of the information for one of the companies that looks interesting to you." Zeke began sifting through his pile. "This place looks so cool," Zeke told me, showing me a Web page printout for Wide, Wonderful World, a tour company. "And I found the name of the guy who manages the tour guides...here it is!" Very quickly, Zeke had collected pieces of data he'd researched about the company.

"Excellent!" I told him. "Now fill out what you can on this company/contact form, and we'll clip the rest of your information to it." A few minutes later Zeke held a neat packet of information about Wide, Wonderful World in his hand. "Now what?" he asked me. "Well, what's the next step you want to take with them?"

"I want to send them a resume and letter of introduction," he answered with confidence. "Sounds good. Make a note of that step in the 'Action steps/record' on the company/contact form." As he did this, I asked him when he planned to prepare the direct-approach package. "I could do that tomorrow," he answered. "That's November

5th," I said, looking at my calendar. "So three-hole punch and file your Wide, Wonderful World packet behind tab #5 in your binder."

"Ah, I see!" Zeke said, confidently snapping the binder ring closed after putting his Wide, Wonderful World information behind tab #5. "You're going to repeat this process for all of your target companies," I told him. "But remember to note the company names and the location of their materials on your master company/contact list, so that you can find what you need easily in the future."

"This will be fun to do, and really helpful," Zeke said, packing up his materials. "It will take me a little time, but already I'm feeling more motivated and in control of succeeding with this search."

Core Courage Concept

Taking the time to get organized can seem tedious…and is it even really worth it? Plus, once you get organized, do you worry that you'll have lost even the little motivation you had to find work in the first place? These are very real concerns. Yet consider this: You want your job search to go as smoothly and as successfully as possible. Any steps that you can take to make your process more efficient will save you from wasting time and getting discouraged. Although the organization system I'm suggesting might seem new and unfamiliar to you, it can make the difference between easy success in your search and frustrating failure. Give it a try!

Confidence Checklist

- ☐ Gather your target list and organization supplies.
- ☐ Fill in your master company/contact list.
- ☐ Create a company/contact info page for all of your target employers.
- ☐ Decide on next step action items for each employer.
- ☐ Choose "due by" dates for your action items.

Chapter 11

Ready, Set, Open Doors to Hidden Opportunities

By now, you might be feeling pretty excited (or terrified) about what you've put in place for yourself: a strong focus for your job search, a list of potential employers, effective documents to support your search plan, and now an organization system that will support your progress. With all of this accomplished, success is right around the corner. Now we're going to kick your job search into even higher gear by having you connect more directly with the potential employers, using the following proven, powerful processes.

Risk It or Run From It?

- **Risk Rating:** These processes are probably the most risky activities recommended in this book, but don't run away yet! Read through the chapter and then decide what you want to implement based on the recommendations.

- **Payoff Potential:** Pretty darn big. Master this step and your future career successes are practically guaranteed.

(continued)

(continued)

- **Time to Complete:** About three minutes per company. (Just three minutes! You can put up with practically anything for three minutes, can't you?)

- **Bailout Strategy:** Well, you can mail the direct-approach packets described in chapter 9 and not follow up, because technically, follow-up is optional (effective, but optional). Or use a less-scary follow-up approach, like e-mail, to connect with the decision makers on your target list.

- **The "20 Percent Extra" Edge:** Very few searchers follow up on materials they've submitted—and you can imagine why. It's scary! Yet you'll be one of the few brave souls who push though their fears to make extraordinary results happen.

- **"Go For It!" Bonus Activity:** Develop an increasing-reward activity for yourself with each follow-up call you make. For instance, tell yourself that for every follow-up action you take, you'll earn five minutes of a massage, or some other motivating reward. This technique helps build even bigger successes!

How to Nudge Your Job Search Successes Even Further Forward

Hooray for you, you're still reading! Although you might not be completely thrilled with all of the suggestions I've made in this book to this point, you're hanging in here and keeping an open mind. Kudos to you! Your willingness to learn new approaches will serve you well. Keep reading to find out about even more strategies to increase your job search successes.

Schedule Your Next Steps

So far you've identified potential employers, created a strong cover letter and resume, and pulled together all of this information into an effective, professional, direct-approach package for each potential employer. Now, after you've stamped, sealed, and sent your envelopes, it's time to put your follow-up plan into action.

Begin by pulling out the job search binder you created in chapter 10, including your completed company/contact info pages. Now, as you begin mailing your direct-approach materials to your target companies, as described in chapter 9, you'll want to file the company/contact info page for each company three business days from the day you sent the package (so if you sent the package on Monday the 21st, file it under tab 24 for Thursday the 24th). Keep in mind that it's important to schedule your follow-up activities at a pace that is doable for you. I suggest starting slow to build momentum. For instance, aim to follow up with just a few companies per day.

Develop Effective Scripts

Now that your packages are mailed and your next-step dates are scheduled, it's time to work on and practice your follow-up scripts.

Panic Point! Are you thinking, "Follow up on the direct-approach packages I've sent? No way!" Okay, okay, I *know* this part is scary. Believe me, my clients struggle with it every day. To them, this feels like the scariest step I ask them to do. But before you get yourself too worked up, keep in mind that technically, you don't even need to do it. (Just be sure that if you don't want to follow up, you remember to remove the line in the letter of introduction that says you'll be contacting your prospective employer. You don't want to look like you don't keep your promises!) For now, however, just take a deep breath and realize that you're just *learning* about how to follow up (no risk in that!), so please keep reading.

Let's say, for example, that on Monday you mailed a direct-approach package to Griffin Simmons, the owner and manager of Wildly Wonderful Adventure Company, a travel service that creates exciting wilderness vacations for clients. After you mailed your envelope, you filed the contact/company info page for Wildly Wonderful Adventure for three days later, on Thursday. Now you want to prepare what you'll say to Griffin when you follow up with him. Here are some scripts that have worked well for others.

Script #1:

> *Mr. Simmons, this is Katy Piotrowski, and I'm following up on a resume and letter I sent to you recently. I wanted to check with you about scheduling a time to talk briefly about ways that I might support your organization. Next Monday morning between 9 and 11, or Tuesday afternoon between 3 and 5, are open for me. My phone number is 970-555-5555, or you can e-mail me at katy@careersolutionsgroup.net. Please let me know what would work best for you. Thank you in advance for your consideration of my request. And if I haven't heard back from you in the next day or so, I'll follow up to make sure you received this message.*

Script #2:

> *Hello Mr. Simmons. This is Katy Piotrowski, and a few days ago I sent a package introducing myself as a potential resource for your organization. As I promised in my letter, I'm following up with you to schedule a brief conversation so that we can meet each other. Times that are open for me in the next few days are Monday morning between 9 and 11, and Tuesday afternoon between 3 and 5. My phone number is 970-555-5555, or you can e-mail me at katy@careersolutionsgroup.net. Please let me know what would work best for you. Thank you in advance for your consideration of my request. If I haven't heard back from you in the next day or so, I'll follow up to make sure you received this message.*

Script #3 (to maintain confidentiality):

> *Hello, Mr. Simmons. I am calling to follow up on a package I mailed you recently. In it, I did not mention my full name, because I want to be respectful to my current employer. I'd like to schedule a brief meeting with you to talk about ways that I might be able to benefit your organization, and I'm hopeful that you will be willing to keep our conversation*

confidential. Times that are open for me in the next few days are Monday morning between 9 and 11, and Tuesday afternoon between 3 and 5. My phone number is 970-555-5555, or you can e-mail me at katy@careersolutionsgroup.net. Please let me know what would work best for you. Thank you in advance for your consideration of my request. If I haven't heard back from you in the next day or so, I'll follow up to make sure you received this message.

Script #4 (e-mail):

Dear Mr. Simmons,

I am writing to follow up on a package I sent to you a few days ago. In it, I expressed interest in meeting briefly to discuss ways that I might benefit your organization. Next week, Monday morning between 9 and 11 and Tuesday afternoon between 3 and 5 are open for me. Please let me know what would work best for you.

Thank you in advance for your consideration of my request. If I haven't heard back from you in the next day or so, I'll follow up to make sure you received this message.

Sincerely,
Katy Piotrowski
(970) 555-5555
katy@careersolutionsgroup.net

You'll notice that both phone and e-mail scripts are provided, so choose the method that feels most comfortable for you.

Practice to Build Confidence and Improve Results

Now, just for fun, practice saying these scripts out loud (I know, I know…you can think of many other ways to have fun, can't you?). I want you to experience what it's actually like to read the scripts.

Most people, when they begin to practice a script like this, have the immediate reaction of, "This feels so awkward! This seems so fake!" Fair enough—it's awkward because you've most likely never done something like this before, and it feels fake because it's a script!

To help you overcome the strangeness of using a script, try the following:

1. Practice saying one of the scripts out loud a few times, word for word.

2. Now edit the script, making small changes so that the wording feels more natural for you.

3. Practice your edited script, out loud, a few more times.

4. Find a friend or job search supporter to practice with, and run through the script at least five more times.

After going through this practice-edit-practice exercise, you'll begin to feel less awkward saying the words, *and* it will feel less like a script because you're putting it into your own words. And so that you're fully prepared, practice and revise the following additional scripts, as potential replies to the responses you might receive from the hiring managers you contact.

Reply to, "We're not hiring right now.":

> *Thank you for that information. I would still very much like to meet you. As you know, situations change, and it could be helpful to know each other as potential resources for the future. Would either Monday morning or Tuesday afternoon work better for you?*

Reply to, "Tell me more about you.":

> *Thank you. I am (brief overview of your work history, education, etc. — check out how to formulate an effective "Tell Me About Yourself" response in* The Career Coward's Guide to Interviewing*). I'd like to get together to share even more information about each other. Would a meeting on Monday morning or Tuesday afternoon work better for you?*

Make the Contact!

Now the moment has arrived. It's time to actually follow through. Your heart is probably pounding, and you're wishing you could transport yourself to another planet and *never* have to actually take this next step.

I know this seems terrifically scary. To help put it in perspective, I'd like you to remember something else you've done in your life that seemed pretty terrifying at the time. For instance, after preparing and submitting the proposal for this book, I needed to follow up with a few editors to see if they were interested. I remember sitting in my office, staring at the follow-up script I'd written, dreading making the calls.

"Just do it," I told myself. Then, in what seemed like slow motion, I watched my hands pick up the phone and dial the first number on my list. My heart was racing as the line rang on the other end. But the first editor I called didn't pick up her phone, so I ended up leaving her a voice mail, reading my script slowly and carefully. Then I hung up the phone and it was over. Whew! I did it!

I was so thrilled with myself that I bounded out of my office and tracked down an office mate to tell her what I'd just done. After getting through the first call, I realized that making the other calls wasn't going to be the death of me, and in fact, the process was building my confidence. The other calls weren't nearly as scary, and eventually I succeeded in landing a book contract (and you're reading evidence of it!).

So think about a scary step you've taken in your life, and remember the courage you showed at that time. Now take a deep breath and get ready to take on another important challenge in your life. The following tips will make the activity of following up even more doable and successful for you.

- **Call when the decision maker is unlikely to answer:** It's perfectly acceptable to leave a voice-mail message, rather than speak directly to your contact. In fact, for many Career Cowards, leaving a voice-mail message feels much more doable. So minimize the chances of having the hiring manager answer by calling before 7:30 a.m. or after 7 p.m. on a business day.

- **Send an e-mail:** In the same way that leaving a voice mail can seem less risky than talking voice-to-voice with a decision maker, sending an e-mail will allow you to communicate your message in a comfortable way. If you're not sure of the hiring manager's e-mail address, you can sometimes determine this by viewing the format of other e-mail addresses on the company's Web site. (If an employee named John Smith has an e-mail address of jsmith@abccorp.com, then an employee named Jane Doe probably has an e-mail address of jdoe@abccorp.com.) Or ask the company receptionist.

- **Use both voice mail and e-mail methods:** I've found the most effective way to get a response from a potential hiring manager is by contacting them twice on the same day. For instance, call and leave a voice-mail message at 7 a.m. on Monday morning, and add the following statement to your message: "I'll also send you an e-mail a little later today to make sure you have my contact information." Then, around noon, send an e-mail. You'll significantly improve your response rate with this "one-two" punch.

- **Motivate yourself in effective ways:** Most likely, you have an idea of what it takes to spur you into action. One of my clients, for instance, would set a timer for two minutes and challenge himself to make a follow-up call before the timer went off. Other job searchers motivate themselves with small rewards, such as a splurge on a coffee or movie rental. Telling myself that I need to "swallow two frogs" each day, and to just get it over with, motivates me. This is a suggestion from motivational speaker Brian Tracy. He recommends that you plan to do two things each day that seem distasteful to you, but that will keep you moving forward.

- **Realize that rejection is only in your mind:** When I first heard this concept, it was a "light bulb" moment for me. Tami Spaulding, a highly successful Colorado real-estate agent, points out that when we receive a negative response to a request, it's our own choice if we decide to treat it as a rejection. Having a hiring manager say, "I don't want to meet with you," is in reality just a string of seven words. It is our own decision to perceive the response as a rejection. So rather than say to yourself, "He rejected me," instead say, "I just received some information. That's all it was—information."

Work Around Gatekeepers

Gatekeepers are the receptionists or phone systems that sometimes make it difficult to connect with your contact. If you need to find your way through the maze of an automated phone system, use the employee directory to obtain the phone extension for the hiring manager. If a receptionist answers, simply ask to be connected to your contact, without a lot of explanation: "Bill Smith or his voice mail, please." If asked about the nature of your call, say that Bill is expecting your call related to a letter he received.

Schedule Your Meeting

Be prepared to offer some potential meeting times when you contact the hiring manager. Instead of saying, "My calendar is wide open," which can make you sound desperate, offer two or three times that will work for you, as in, "Tuesday or Thursday afternoon between 2 and 4 are open for me." If those times don't work for the hiring manager, ask her to suggest a few possibilities.

Why It's Worth Doing

Companies hire people, not resumes. At some point, it's important to connect personally with hiring managers. Making a follow-up phone call or sending an e-mail allows the hiring manager to begin knowing you as an individual. Plus, following up with hiring managers builds your courage muscles, one small call at a time!

Career Champ Profile: Marcus

Marcus's job search seemed dead in the water. He'd been hunting for five months and had landed only a few job interviews. The process of waiting for interesting job ads to show up online and in the publications he read was maddeningly slow. For three weeks in a row, at our weekly meetings, I encouraged Marcus to mail some direct-approach packages to potential employers. Finally he agreed. "There are about 10 petroleum companies I've wanted to connect with," he told me. "This might be a great way to do it."

The first week, Marcus mailed five direct-approach packages to each VP of Finance—the person he would be reporting to—at the petroleum companies on his list. Three days after he'd mailed the packages, he followed up with a phone call to each, requesting a brief meeting. He was unable to get past the receptionist at three of the companies, and ended up leaving a message for his contact instead. But he was able to connect directly with the VPs at the other two companies. One of them said he was too busy to meet with Marcus, but that he'd keep his resume on file. The other VP very willingly set up a meeting. Marcus filled me in on the details when we met the next week.

"This guy was great," Marcus began. "It turns out we both love baseball, so we talked about that for a while. I went through my agenda, just like you and I talked about, and when we got to the part of showing him my target list, he was so helpful. He gave me names of four people he knows at other companies on my list. He also gave me information for a recruiter in the petroleum industry who might be very helpful to me. Then he told me about two other companies I didn't even know about, and gave me contact names there. Plus he offered to call all of them to give me an introduction. That's seven great contacts! And that's not all. He also told me about a job they might be filling at his company in the next three months, and he's going to keep me in mind for it.

"Katy, I'll confess that I didn't think this direct-approach stuff would work. But I'm a believer now! I don't see why every job searcher wouldn't look for work this way. It makes so much sense, and it's so much more fun than waiting for those stupid ads!"

Core Courage Concept

In your career, connecting directly with hiring managers to say, "Here I am, and my talents and experience might be useful to you," is one of the most challenging steps you'll ever take. Yet, as is true with many risks we take in life, the bigger the chance you take, the larger the reward you stand to gain. If following up with hiring managers freaks you out, consider yourself normal. But if you want to take your career to the next level, challenge yourself to push beyond your career cowardice to achieve extraordinary results.

Confidence Checklist

- ☐ Schedule your next steps.
- ☐ Develop effective scripts.
- ☐ Practice to build confidence and improve results.
- ☐ Make the contact!
- ☐ Work around gatekeepers.
- ☐ Schedule your meeting.

Chapter 12

Link Up Through Other Effective (and Less Scary) Avenues

In the last few chapters, we've been talking about how to connect with potential employers by approaching them directly. Although it's effective, I know that this can be a pretty scary activity, especially for Career Cowards. So in this chapter, I'll give you several ideas for successfully meeting people who can you move your job search forward, through activities that might feel more comfortable to you.

Risk It or Run From It?

- **Risk Rating:** Mid-level risk. Nothing in here will kill you, but it might make your heart pound a little.

- **Payoff Potential:** At the risk of sounding cliché, it's not what you know, but who you know.

- **Time to Complete:** A few minutes to a few hours, depending on what you select.

- **Bailout Strategy:** Stick with responding to job ads and sending out direct-approach materials. You'll get decent

(continued)

(continued)

results even without using some of these activities. But just for fun, you might try one or two, just to build your courage muscle and to improve your odds of a highly successful job search.

- **The "20 Percent Extra" Edge:** Study after study shows that the jobs uncovered through personal connections are the highest-quality opportunities available. Finding ways to connect with supporters will greatly improve your chances of locating and landing great positions.

- **"Go For It!" Bonus Activity:** Look for ways to help other people with connections, such as assisting a fellow job searcher in finding a contact at one of her target companies. You'll see firsthand how rewarding it can be to pass on the support.

How to Make Helpful Job Search Connections Through Fun, Doable Activities

Even though the idea might terrify you, you know that connecting with others can significantly improve your job search results. The trick is to find methods that are comfortable and that you're willing to do. One or more of the following ideas is bound to fit your style.

Create a List of People You Already Know

Most people, when asked, "What about contacting people in your own circle of friends and acquaintances?" quickly jump to the conclusion, "I don't really know anyone—or the people I know aren't people I'd necessarily want to involve in my job search." Okay, fair enough…but humor me for a minute. Just for fun, I want you to make a list of people who fit into the following groups, aiming to list at least five people within each category. Just pick up your pen and make a list:

- Friends

- Family members

- Coworkers, past and present

- Bosses, past and present

- Teachers, past and present

- Clients, vendors, or businesspeople you work with regularly

- Members of clubs, churches, or associations you participate in

- Other people in your address book who don't fit into any of these categories

Chances are you've just created a list of 40 or more people in your personal circle who might be able to

- Provide you a reference.

- Give you pros and cons feedback about the organizations on your target list.

- Connect you to someone within the companies you're researching.

- Suggest other businesses you should add to your target list.

- Be on the lookout for job opportunities that fit your career goals.

- Give you a boost of self-belief and moral support when you're feeling frustrated with your search.

Down the line, you might decide to link up with some of these contacts, so keep your personal-circle list handy.

Hook into Hobby, Service, and Professional Groups

Like to ski, knit, or whatever? Enjoy volunteering at nonprofit organizations? Pride yourself on keeping up with cutting-edge developments in your field? If so, it's very likely that a group exists that you would enjoy connecting with and that could also help you advance your job search.

Many people (especially Career Cowards) initially cringe at the idea of being a part of a group. "I'm not a joiner!" they adamantly say. Yet once they hit upon the idea of a group that seems strongly interesting to them, they're a little more open to the idea.

For instance, one of my past clients is an avid mountain biker, and he was job searching for work as a programmer. When I suggested that he get involved with a professional association of programmers, he wasn't interested. Yet when I offered another idea about joining a club of local mountain bikers, he was open to giving it a try.

So think about which activities are meaningful and fun for you, and then ask yourself, "Which groups of people get together to discuss or participate in activities involving this topic?" Input keywords on a search engine to locate potential organizations, such as "volunteer opportunities to teach adults to read," or "professional association meeting planners Colorado." The reference librarian at your local library can also help you locate potential clubs and associations. Once you begin your investigation, it's likely that you'll discover a number of possibilities.

Then, for fun, attend the group meetings or activities once or twice. You don't need to commit yourself forever—just visit a group once or twice to see what you think. If it fits your style and interests, hooray! If not, no big deal…at least you gave it a try. But if you are able to find one or more groups that are a match for you, participate regularly and actively. Join committees and find ways to contribute. As you do, you'll discover that often the other members can be helpful resources in your job search.

Panic Point! Worry about what you'd do or say at a group meeting, or if others in the group would be friendly toward you? I agree! Meeting new people can be intimidating. Regarding what to say, one of the best strategies is to ask lots of questions of the people you meet, such as, "How long have you been a member of this group? What do you enjoy about it?" and so on (and check out the F.O.R.D. technique in chapter 13 for other small-talk ideas). This approach shifts the focus from you to them, and most people are very happy to talk about themselves. Another idea is to e-mail the group organizer ahead of time to let her know you'll be coming and that you'd like her to introduce you to a few people when you arrive. Finally, regarding the friendliness of the group, I predict that you'll be pleasantly surprised at how welcoming members will be. In my experience, members of volunteer, hobby, and professional organizations are usually passionate about the focus of the group and are eager to meet and involve others who feel the same way.

Participate in Job Search Support Groups

Similar to hobby, service, or professional organizations, the members of job search support groups can help you move your job search forward by providing information, leads, and encouragement. They might be coordinated independently or run by a local job service organization.

Typically, job search support groups meet one or more times each month. The meetings include informing each other about job search objectives, learning about and practicing effective job hunting techniques, and troubleshooting job search roadblocks. Most groups allow job hunters to participate for free or for a minimal fee. To locate job search support groups near you, input the keywords, "job search support group (your city)" into a search engine, or phone your local job service center for suggestions.

Partner with Employment Services and Recruiters

Deep down, most of us wish that we had a Career Fairy who would fly around locating great job opportunities and then gently drop them in our lap for our consideration. Although the Career Fairy doesn't exist (as far as I'm aware), there are professionals whose job it is to link candidates with job opportunities. These professionals are called recruiters.

Many people mistakenly believe that it's a recruiter's role to find positions for job searchers. This, however, isn't true. Rather, *it's the role of a recruiter to locate personnel resources for companies.* This might seem like a minor difference, but in reality, it's huge. Here's why: A recruiter gets paid by an employer company to find candidates for a job opening. The recruiter's loyalty is to the company, not to the job searcher. *Unless a recruiter sees how your background might be a fit for a position he or she is filling, you are of very little interest to him.*

For this reason, if you choose to connect with recruiters, it's important that you approach them from *their* perspective, rather than from yours. The following scripts demonstrate "wrong way" and "right way" methods.

Wrong way:

> *Mr. Recruiter, I'm job searching. What positions do you have open?*

Right way:

> *Mr. Recruiter, I'm job searching for a position as a (state your job search focus). If my background is a fit for one of the positions you're filling, I'd like to provide you with information about me. If my background isn't a fit for one of your searches, I'd like to be on the lookout for other candidates that might be good resources for you.*

To find recruiters that fit your specialty, ask the membership coordinator at your professional association for ideas. You can also connect with employment agencies, listed under "Employment Services" in the Yellow Pages, to locate potential employment services and recruiters.

A note about employment services as compared to professional recruiters: Employment services—such as Manpower, Adecco, Apple One, and so on—are typically focused on filling positions locally, from entry-level openings to specialty technical positions.

Professional recruiters, often working independently, are usually focused on filling higher-level (CEO, VP, and so on) or more specialized positions, recruiting from nationwide or worldwide candidate pools. At one time, they might be supporting companies located in Bangkok, Buenos Aires, and Boston. For this reason, candidates need to be open to relocation.

Connect to Others Electronically

If the idea of making connections electronically, rather than face to face, seems more comfortable to you (and it does for many Career Cowards), here are some ideas for e-connecting:

- E-mail individuals in your personal network about your job search goals and ask them for ideas and support (for more details on this idea, see chapter 13).

- Consider setting up a profile on an online networking site to advance your job search. Sites such as LinkedIn and Ryze allow you to create a profile about your background and career goals, and then to connect to others through a variety of electronic activities. There are several levels of involvement, depending on how active you want to be. Most online networking services allow you to join for no charge and add additional membership benefits for a fee, if you choose. Most of the job searchers I know who have created their initial profiles are pleasantly surprised to discover that they already have several potential connections, as they locate a number of former coworkers and classmates.

As with most things in life, the more effort you put into your online networking efforts, the more rewards you'll see. Don't expect to post your profile and then to have a landslide of connections just come rolling in. You'll need to invest a little more effort. For instance, look for opportunities to support others in your network, and in return, you'll find others will be more active in supporting you.

Why It's Worth Doing

Way back in chapter 2, I talked about how studies show that one of the most effective avenues for job searchers is through connections with others. And because fewer than 10 percent of job hunters actively use people-connecting activities in their job search, those who put even a little effort into these activities quickly see positive results. So finding some avenues to meet and share your job search goals with others makes sense.

Plus, if you've been job searching the same way throughout your career (and have been frustrated with the results), you owe it to yourself to try something different.

Career Champ Profile: Blaine

Blaine, a Web marketing specialist, had worked for a publishing company for seven years and had enjoyed his experience there for most of that time. But then the company was sold and the culture of the new organization was different. Blaine wasn't as happy there anymore and decided to find new work.

"And while I'm at it," he told me, "I'd like to move into an industry that's more interesting and meaningful to me. Publishing is okay, but I think I can find a better fit." After exploring some career change ideas as described in *The Career Coward's Guide to Changing Careers*, Blaine decided to seek work as a marketing specialist with a company focused on sustainability and "green" operating practices, in line with his strong interest in maintaining a healthy planet. Then he put together a list of target companies and began job searching.

"Let's brainstorm some ways for you to connect with people, to make your job hunting activities even more successful," I said. As a first idea, I suggested participating in a marketing association. "Weeeeellllllll, I don't know," Blaine replied. "I went to one of those meetings about a year ago and really didn't feel like I fit in."

"Okay, let's keep thinking," I said. We then brainstormed a list of several ideas, using Google to input keywords such as *sustainability, association,* and *northern Colorado* to investigate local clubs and organizations. An association called Green Drinks popped up on my screen.

"What's that?" Blaine asked, leaning in closer to my screen. We clicked on the link and discovered that Green Drinks is a group of local professionals who meet at a bar once each month to socialize and to discuss ways to promote and advance the use of sustainability practices in northern Colorado. There was a meeting scheduled for the coming Thursday, at 5 p.m. "Oh, cool!" Blaine exclaimed, excited.

He attended the meeting and reported to me the next week. "Wow, it was great! I met about 15 people who are involved in a variety of sustainability activities around here. It was super-energizing, talking about things that are important to me and to them. And I agreed to help out on a committee that's putting together a new Web page for the group. I'm getting experience in the industry, meeting people who can be on the lookout for opportunities that might fit my background, and it's fun! This is a people-connecting activity I'm willing to do."

Core Courage Concept

Connecting with others is an activity that can go very well...or very poorly. Because meeting new people can feel pretty risky, many Career Cowards would rather not chance it at all. Yet in reality, expanding your circle of contacts usually leads to a positive result, plus it can go a long way toward helping you achieve your career goals. The trick is in finding a people-connecting activity that you're willing to do—and experimenting with several ideas until you find one that fits for you.

Confidence Checklist

☐ Create a list of people you already know.

☐ Hook into hobby, service, and professional groups.

☐ Participate in job search support groups.

☐ Connect to others electronically.

Chapter 13

Expand Your Job Possibilities Through People

With all the discussion about connecting with people in the last few chapters, you might be asking yourself, "Then what? What do I say to these people I meet? How can we help each other?" That's what we'll cover in detail in this chapter, so get ready to learn how personal connections can advance your job search in amazing ways.

Risk It or Run From It?

- **Risk Rating:** Although the connecting-with-others part might feel pretty scary, these steps are actually of only mid-range risk. I'll give you a step-by-step formula to take the guesswork out of what to say and do.

- **Payoff Potential:** Excellent! Personal connections can be your strongest job search tool.

- **Time to Complete:** Plan on investing 15–60 minutes per personal connection.

- **Bailout Strategy:** Rather than the one-on-one activities described in this chapter, use some of the suggestions covered in chapter 12. And keep in mind that you don't need to

---

(continued)

(continued)

connect with others—in fact, most job searchers don't. However, personal connections consistently yield the best job opportunities, so even if you invest just a little effort, you'll begin to see excellent results.

- **The "20 Percent Extra" Edge:** Attempting to connect with others is a daunting task—and not knowing what you'll say is especially scary! Having a proven, step-by-step agenda to follow will increase your confidence and improve your results.

- **"Go For It!" Bonus Activity:** Create a "network net" record of the contacts you make and how quickly your circle of supporters grows. This visual picture can serve as concrete evidence of your progress.

How to Link Up with Others to Improve Your Job Search Results

Now I'll introduce you to several small, doable activities that will allow you to connect with people to move your job search forward—from arranging a time to talk, to sending a thank-you note after your conversation.

Create Calling Cards

As you begin connecting with others, you'll want to be able to exchange contact information so that you can follow up with each other later. Business cards are the most common and accepted method for doing this. However, because you're job searching, you might not have a business card to use…plus, it's inappropriate to present a business card paid for by your employer for job hunting. The solution to this problem is to create your own calling cards, in the same size and look as simple business cards, imprinted with your contact info. Here's an example:

Katy Piotrowski
(970) 555-5555
katyp@gmail.com

You'll notice that I've included only my name, phone number, and e-mail address. Technically, this is the only information you need. I recommend *not* including a job title or career objective, such as "Marketing Manager" or "Software Programmer" on your card. Otherwise, the recipient might mistakenly think that you are working as a consultant in your own business, instead of searching for a job.

Cards like this can be created using a template provided in your word-processing software and printed on business-card paper available at office-supply stores. Or have them prepared for you at your local photocopy shop, or online at a business card Web site such as www.vistaprint.com. Aim to have about 200 to 300 printed.

Set Up One-on-One Conversations

At group events, such as professional association meetings and volunteer activities, it can be difficult to orchestrate a meaningful conversation with another person—there's just too much going on! Plus the top priority at events like these is the planned activity, whether that means working through the meeting agenda or making progress on a project. Although your job search is important, it's not *the* most important activity at the event, and trying to get 15 minutes of a participant's undivided attention to talk about your job search isn't appropriate.

For this reason, it works best to arrange a separate conversation with people you want to talk with further. Let's say, for example, that you meet Heath Williams while volunteering on a community gardening project. As you and he are digging in the dirt, making small talk about the weather and worms, the two of you seem to hit it off. Now you'd like to set up a one-on-one conversation with him to get to know him better and to brainstorm about your job search. As you wrap up the day's project, you could say,

Heath, I've enjoyed meeting you today. I'd like to get to know you better, and to brainstorm some ideas with you about a job search I'm conducting. Would you be willing to meet me for coffee sometime in the next few weeks?

After he agrees (and he most likely will—most people do), give him your calling card, collect a card from him (if he doesn't have a card, have him write his info on the back of one of yours), and then offer to follow up to arrange the details.

This same script, with minor modifications, would work well for setting up a meeting with someone you already know. In this case, Cybil:

Cybil, it's been a while since we've talked, and I'd like to get together to catch up. I'd also like to brainstorm some ideas with you about a job search I'm conducting. Would you be willing to meet me for coffee sometime in the next few weeks?

Panic Point! Does the idea of requesting a meeting with someone to talk about your job search make you feel like you're "using" your contact? Being perceived as someone who "uses" others is probably the biggest reason why most Career Cowards don't connect more when job searching. No one likes to feel used! However, *most people understand the importance of connecting with others while job hunting.* They know that they, too, might very likely be in your shoes at some time in the future...then *they'll* want to be able to make the same request of *you!* (This is also known as, "I'll scratch your back, so you'll scratch mine.") If you treat your contacts with respect, most people will view your request to brainstorm ideas about your job search as a win-win opportunity. So push through your fear about coming across as a "user," and instead look at this as an opportunity to establish a valuable, productive connection between you and your contact!

When you do follow up to schedule a conversation, have a plan in mind: If you want to meet in person, be ready to suggest a time and location. If you want to talk on the phone, have your calendar handy. And be sure to reemphasize your purpose, which is setting up a 15 to 30-minute conversation to find out ways that you can support each other, including brainstorming ideas about your job search.

Master the "You, Me, We" Conversation Agenda

After you've gotten over the hurdle of asking for and scheduling a time to talk, the next big question is...what will you talk about? Following is a tried-and-true agenda, one that I call, "You, Me, We." It will provide you step-by-step details for what to say and when to say it.

This concept originally came from job search expert Daniel Porot as an outline for cover letters. I've adapted it as a highly effective agenda for job search brainstorming conversations. To show you how it works, imagine that you (we'll call you Chris for this example) have arranged to meet Kendra (someone you met at a professional association meeting) for coffee. Your conversation will follow this basic outline:

- **You:** In this initial part of the meeting, you will focus on Kendra, as in "Kendra, I am going to first focus on *you*" (that's where the "you" pronoun comes in). This part of the meeting should take somewhere between 5 and 10 minutes.

- **Me:** In the second part of the meeting, you will shift the focus back to you, as in, "Now I'm going to spend a few minutes talking about what's going on with *me*." This will take you five minutes or less.

- **We:** In this last part of the conversation, you and Kendra will be brainstorming together—that's the "we" part. This segment should take five minutes or less.

Now that we have the pronouns straight (You–Kendra, Me–Chris, We–Kendra and Chris together), I'll cover these sections in more detail.

The "You" Part of the Conversation

The purpose of the "you" segment in the agenda is to connect with your contact in a meaningful way and to get the conversation off to a good start. By focusing first on Kendra, you show her that she's important to you, and you increase your chances of her supporting you later in the conversation. My favorite "you" focus strategy is the F.O.R.D. technique, an acronym standing for *Family, Occupation, Recreation,* and *Dreams.* Asking questions about these topics allows you to focus successfully on your contact. Here are some examples:

- **Family:** "Where are you from originally? Do you have family in this area?"

- **Occupation:** "Tell me how things are going for you in your work. What aspects of your job are particularly exciting or challenging for you right now?"

- **Recreation:** "What do you do for fun? Been on any interesting trips or vacations recently?"

- **Dreams:** "Where do you hope to take things in the future? Any exciting projects or developments that you're aiming for?"

Feel free to modify the F.O.R.D. questions to come up with some that feel comfortable to you. And realize that you don't need to ask your contact about *every* topic within the F.O.R.D. acronym—it's just a handy memory technique to help you keep the conversation going smoothly. And believe me, it *will* go smoothly, provided that you ask good questions and then *listen* to Kendra's responses. Here are a few tips to ensure that you're listening successfully:

- **Make eye contact** (although it's perfectly fine to shift your eyes away from Kendra occasionally—you don't want her to feel like you're glaring at her!). If you're uncomfortable looking directly at Kendra, look at the space between her eyes instead.

- **Truly focus on what's being said.** One of the biggest mistakes people make in conversing with others is thinking about how they're going to respond before the other person has even finished talking. Don't *worry* about what you're going to say next, and instead listen intently to Kendra. Chances are very good that as you listen, you'll come up with another question to ask her, allowing you to keep the conversation going. And if there's a little pause in the conversation, as you think of your next question, that's okay, too.

- **Avoid jumping in with your own "stuff."** It's so tempting to want to share your own experiences when talking with someone else, as in, "Oh, I once had a dog, too!" Remember, the first part of this conversation is about *Kendra,* so keep the focus on her. Your turn will come shortly.

After you've spent 5 to 10 minutes learning about Kendra and what's going on in her life, you'll then need to move into the "me" part of the conversation. A good way to segue this transition is to look at your timepiece (your watch, your cell phone, or the clock on the wall) and say:

> *Kendra, I want to make good use of your time, so I'm going to now tell you a little bit about what's going on with me....*

This is a *very* handy statement to master, because otherwise you might end up spending the entire conversation on the "you" part of the agenda and never get to the "me" or "we" segments.

The "Me" Part of the Conversation

So you've just spent the last 5 to 10 minutes catching up on Kendra's life. Now it's time to move into the "me" part of the agenda to bring Kendra up to speed on what's going on with you and your job search activities.

Panic Point! Nervous about putting the focus on yourself for fear that you'll come across as self-centered? Again, this is a *very* typical Career Coward fear. But keep in mind that a) you've just focused intently on your contact for 5 to 10 minutes, so now it's *your* turn, and b) your contact is *expecting* you to talk about your job search, because you mentioned it when you set up the meeting! Plus, you'll be keeping this part of the conversation to five minutes or less, so it will be over before you know it.

In the "Me" part of your conversation, you want to aim to cover these three points:

1. Clearly state your job search goal, as in "I'm looking for a position as a branch manager with a bank."

2. Briefly share your resume and point out a few highlights in your background related to your job search goal. For instance, "Kendra, here's a copy of my resume for you to have for your records. As you can see, in my last position, I managed the Greenwood branch for First Money Keepers. I was successful in that position, and grew the bank by 75 percent within two years…." Your goal with this activity is to paint a picture for Kendra about what you're great at and what you want to do more of in the future, using one to two specific examples from your past.

3. Ask Kendra to keep you in mind if she learns of any job opportunities that match your job search goals.

Note: If you need additional ideas about how to describe a few key pieces of your background, check out *The Career Coward's Guide to Interviewing* for suggestions.

That's it! Once you cover these three "me" pieces, you can transition to the last part of the conversation—the "we." A smooth way to move into this portion of the agenda is to say something like this:

Now that you know a little about what I'm looking for, I'd love to brainstorm some next steps with you....

The "We" Part of the Conversation

You're in the home stretch now! Now you just need to wrap up your conversation with a successful "we" discussion. Here's how this part of the conversation goes:

1. Pull out two copies of your target list (the one you developed in chapter 4—only make this a simplified version, listing only the company names), hand one to Kendra, and say, "I'd like to get your input on the following organizations I'm researching."

2. Ask, "What do you know about any of these companies—pros and cons, updates about what's happening with them, people I should talk to, and so on?"

3. Listen and make notes as Kendra offers some thoughts. For instance, she might say, "Well, XYZ Bank just upgraded their Information Technology capabilities. I have a friend, Bob, who is a friend of the bank's president, and he worked with them on setting up their new system. Oh, and ABC Savings is supposedly going to open a new branch soon. My girlfriend Maya is an architect and is working with them on the building design. But stay away from LMNOP Trust Bank. I hear the company's owner is a bear to work under." As she's talking, show interest, and resist the urge to "Yeah, but..." her ideas, as in "Yeah, but I'm not interested in ABC Savings because..." If you "Yeah, but..." Kendra's ideas, she'll want to stop offering them.

4. Ask for clarification and confirm next steps. For instance, "Kendra, you mentioned that XYZ Bank just upgraded their IT capability. Do you know what system they chose?" And, "You said that your friends Bob and Maya know about what's happening with some of the banks in the area. I'd love to talk

with them and learn more about the organizations I'm researching. Would it be okay if I contacted them and mentioned that I talked with you?"

5. Thank her for her time, and provide her with your calling card.

6. Follow up with a written (e-mail or hardcopy) thank you note within 48 hours.

That's it! Not *too* terrible, is it? And now that you know how these "You, Me, We" conversations work, find out how you can keep your connections moving forward successfully.

Follow Up to Maximize Your Opportunities

As demonstrated in the "You, Me, We" conversation with Kendra, it's very likely that once you begin to connect with people, your list of contacts will begin to grow. For example, Kendra can introduce you to Bob and Maya, allowing you to set up and conduct "You, Me, We" conversations with each of them. And they can connect you to others, and so on. Within just a few weeks, the list of people you know connected to your target companies could be much bigger!

To set up your next round of meetings, use the same script described earlier, only this time, mention the person who referred you:

> *Hello, Bob. I was referred to you by Kendra. She mentioned that you have some knowledge of the local banking industry, and I'm hoping that we can meet to brainstorm some ideas about a job search I'm conducting. Would you be willing to meet me for coffee sometime in the next few weeks?*

If you follow the "You, Me, We" process with these new contacts, your group of supporters—as well as the job opportunities you'll learn about—will continue to grow.

Why It's Worth Doing

In my role as career counselor, I've had the opportunity to observe the ups and downs of thousands of job searchers as they hunt for work. Over time, I've noticed that those searchers fall into two very distinct groups: those who regularly connect with others for ideas and support (about 10 percent of them), and those who don't (the other 90 percent). The results of each of these groups are markedly different.

For those who connect very little with others, their attitudes about their job search are almost always doom and gloom. They frequently say things like, "There just aren't any opportunities out there. I'll never find what I want."

Yet those who frequently link up with people as part of their job search activities seem to have the exact opposite experience. They are energized and optimistic about their search, and frequently comment that there are so many job possibilities, they're not sure how they'll be able to juggle them all.

This comparison might seem pretty dramatic to you, but the phenomenon I describe is true—and the primary difference from what I can see is the act of reaching out to others. It's as if every person you connect with multiplies the power and energy of your job search. In fact, Michael Farr, author of *The Very Quick Job Search*, estimates that *40 percent of unemployment would go away if connections between people were better.*

Yes, I know, connecting with others is an unknown, and for most job searchers, it's a task they dread so much they simply won't do it. Yet if connecting through others will significantly speed your success in finding work, isn't it at least worth experimenting with?

Career Champ Profile: Chelsea

Though she was nervous about it, Chelsea knew that she'd greatly increase her chances for landing a fantastic job if she started connecting more with people. So she mustered up some courage and attended the monthly meeting of the local manufacturing managers association. She found herself sitting next to Wendy, the owner of a local brewery. They made small talk during the breaks in the meeting, and at the end, exchanged cards. "Would you be willing to get together for coffee sometime?" Chelsea asked Wendy. "I'm in the middle of a job search and I'd love to brainstorm some ideas with you." Wendy quickly agreed, and Chelsea e-mailed her the next day to arrange a time to get together. Wendy suggested that they meet the following Tuesday at 10 a.m. at her office.

I saw Chelsea the day after her meeting with Wendy. "How did it go?" I asked her. "It was really amazing," Chelsea began. "I followed the 'You, Me, We' outline, and it worked great. And when I showed Wendy my target list, that's when things really started to happen. She walked us both over to her controller's office, and the two of them brainstormed several ideas for me—other companies to consider, people to talk to…. I walked out of there with eight contacts! You know that I've dreaded the idea of connecting with others about my job search. But now that I've started doing it, I can see how much it's going to help. I'm feeling much more optimistic about my job search than I was just a few days ago."

Core Courage Concept

Connecting with others is probably the most difficult step you'll encounter in your job search. Unless you do it regularly, meeting new people can feel especially stressful. Yet every person you involve in your job search can serve as a valuable resource for you, serving as eyes and ears on the lookout for great opportunities. So even if you set up just one meeting, give yourself a chance to see what can happen from the power of connecting with others. Your career will thank you!

Confidence Checklist

- ☐ Create calling cards.
- ☐ Set up one-on-one conversations.
- ☐ Master the "You, Me, We" conversation agenda.
- ☐ Follow up to maximize your opportunities.

Part 3

Track, Tweak, and Maximize Your Job Search Results

Chapter 14

Maximize Your Job Search Results with Minimum Effort

Believe it or not, you now have the power to achieve awesome job search results easily and efficiently! Over the last several chapters, you've learned about the most effective activities for connecting with employers who are the best fit for your background. And now that you know all the steps involved, you're going to learn how to put together these pieces so that you can dance through your search smoothly.

Risk It or Run From It?

- **Risk Rating:** Getting your new routine in place might feel awkward for a few days, but other than that, there's no risk involved.

- **Payoff Potential:** You'll learn how to gain the most from your job search efforts, with the least amount of effort involved.

- **Time to Complete:** A few minutes to set up your plan, a few days to get into the swing of your new routine, and then whatever time you decide to invest in your search each day.

(continued)

(continued)

> - **Bailout Strategy:** This step is an "extra"—but a very valuable one. In reality, you could skip it and conduct your search freeform. But it wouldn't hurt for you to spend a few minutes reading through my suggestions. Chances are you'll find ways to be more efficient with less effort in this chapter.
>
> - **The "20 Percent Extra" Edge:** When you diet, you track your eating to better control the outcome of your results. Similarly, when you create a plan for and track your job search activities, you're more likely to stay on track and achieve your goals.
>
> - **"Go For It!" Bonus Activity:** To help keep you on track, create and post your job search plan and schedule in a place where you can refer to it often.

How to Achieve the Most from Your Job Search (with the Least Effort Possible!)

A few years ago, my girlfriend Maury invited me to an exercise class. "I think you'd really like it," she said. Even though I already had an exercise routine that I was reasonably pleased with, I have great respect for Maury, so I decided to give it a try. So on a Sunday, I met Maury for my very first yoga class.

To summarize my experience, I *hated* it. I didn't know any of the poses, and most of what the instructor asked us to do felt goofy to me. After class, I told my husband I thought yoga was ridiculous, and that I was *never* going back.

But a few days later, a small voice in my head kept saying to me, "Katy, that yoga stuff was really good for your body. You should do it again." Even though I hated feeling so awkward in that first class, I intuitively could tell that the stretches, balances, and strength-building exercises would be helpful to me. So I went back…and I've been doing two or three sessions of yoga each week ever since.

Now I have a fitness routine that's more efficient and enjoyable than anything else I've done in my 20+ years of exercising—but I almost threw it away because my first experience was so unpleasant. As you get your new job search habits in place, you might have the same kind of negative reaction that I did to my first experiences with yoga: Initially, it will probably feel uncomfortable, but a small voice in your head will be saying, "Stick with this…it makes sense." Then, before you know it, you'll find yourself executing a smooth and successful search that gets you the results you want.

Calculate About How Long Your Job Search Should Take

How long will your job search take? For years, specialists in my line of work have used the guideline of one month of searching for every $10,000 in income you expect to earn annually. So if you're aiming for positions that pay about $80,000 per year, it will probably take you about eight months to find a job. In general, I find this guideline holds pretty true.

However, I've also discovered that if you put more time into your search, especially in those activities that typically generate better results, you can shorten this estimated timeline significantly. For instance, based on my observations, most job hunters invest less than an hour per day in their searches, or about six hours each week. They might be working full time, and an hour is all they can squeeze in. Those are the job searchers, I've found, for whom the one-month-per-$10,000 guideline holds pretty true.

Yet when you devote more time to your search—up to six hours *per day*, for example—you can speed things up quite a bit. In this case, you could calculate one hour of job searching for every $400 you aim to earn annually. An $80,000-per-year position, for instance, would probably take about 200 hours of job searching to find. And if you're investing about six hours each weekday, or 24 hours each week, chances are pretty good that you could wrap up a search in about two months!

Panic Point! Are you having a panic attack over how long your job search will take? That's understandable...who *really* wants to put in hour after hour of job searching, anyway? No one! However, consider this: When you've job-searched before, you've put in hour after hour of effort, but unless you added it all up, you weren't aware of the time you'd invested. Now I'm asking you to calculate your estimated timeline so that you can plan your activities more efficiently. Then, rather than think, "Yikes! This is going to be a lot of work!" you can instead look at it as, "Okay, so this is about how long it will take. I'm going to be as efficient as possible to get it completed."

So determine about how much time you can put into your search each week, and from there, you can calculate the estimated job hunting timeline.

Set Up a Job Search Plan That Works for You

Now that you understand the steps involved in executing a successful job search, as well as about how many hours of job searching you'll need to invest, you'll want to set up a plan that works with your schedule and maximizes your results. Following are sample plans designed to support job hunting full time (six hours per day), half time (three hours per day), and part time (one hour per day). Each plan factors in activities from the three most successful job search avenues: responding to job ads, approaching companies directly, and connecting with others.

Full-Time Job Search Plan

If you're not working and have more time in your schedule to devote to effective job hunting activities, the following plan might work well for you. It's based on six hours of job searching activities for each weekday. Feel free to shuffle the hours around, depending on your personal preferences, to take advantage of when you have the most energy throughout the day.

- **Hour 1:** Review the plan you created at the end of the day yesterday. Get dressed appropriately for the activities planned for today. Make any before-business-hours calls you need to make, including following up on job applications you submitted recently (see chapter 8 for tips).

- **Hour 2:** Meet a contact for an energizing "You, Me, We" coffee meeting (see chapter 13 for details). This might be a contact from your own circle of supporters, a recruiter connected to your specialty, or a referral from someone you've linked up with recently.

- **Hour 3:** Spend 60 minutes reading classifieds and surfing job and company Web sites to identify any new openings. Create application packages in response to the opportunities you uncover, using the strategies described in chapter 7.

- **Hour 4:** Review the list of target companies you created in chapter 4. Prepare and send two or three "Consider Me!" packages (see chapter 9 for how-tos).

- **Hour 5:** Connect with one or more individuals through e-mail, phone calls, or by attending a group event to inform others about your job search goals, and to make new contacts (several ideas for these activities are described in chapter 12). Schedule any upcoming "You, Me, We" conversations, aiming for an average of one per business day.

- **Hour 6:** Review your activities and results for the day. Update your job searching binder and master company/contact list (described in chapter 10). Spend time researching any new contacts or company information you need to maximize your results for tomorrow, and add information to your company/contact info pages. Send e-mails or make phone calls to confirm any meetings you have set up for the next day. Make any after-hours calls you need to make. Create your plan for tomorrow.

Panic Point! Does this hour-by-hour plan seem too structured and "packed" to you? Are you starting to feel stressed over all of the activities I'm suggesting? Okay, take a few deep breaths and realize that this is just a *plan*. You won't need to implement it all right away. Over time, you can do a little more each day, building momentum as you go. But don't feel as if you need to jump in completely from day one.

Half-Time Job Search Plan

If you don't have all day to devote to job searching, but could put in at least three hours, this plan would work for you.

- **Hour 1:** Develop a job search plan for the day. Dress yourself appropriately for the day's activities. Make any before-hours phone calls. Conduct any additional company or contact research needed. Update your company/contact information pages. Send out at least one "Consider me!" package to a company on your target list.

- **Hour 2:** Log on to your favorite job and company Web sites to check out any new job postings. Prepare responses to any ads that match your job search goals.

- **Hour 3:** Spend this hour connecting with others, either by meeting someone for coffee for a "You, Me, We" conversation, attending an association or hobby group meeting, or phoning people in your circle to schedule get-togethers or exchange information over the phone.

Part-Time Job Search Plan

If you're already engaged in a full-time activity, such as a job or caring for a family member, you'll most likely have less time to devote to job search activities—but you can still make good progress! The following plan is set up to allow you to fit in six hours of effective job search activities throughout your week, in a schedule that is flexible for your needs. Rearrange the recommended daily activities to suit your schedule for the week.

- **Day 1:** Create a job search plan for the week. Spend time researching any needed company or contact information to support your plan. Update your company/contact information pages.

- **Day 2:** Meet a contact for an energizing "You, Me, We" coffee meeting.

- **Day 3:** Spend 60 minutes reading classifieds and surfing job and company Web sites to identify any new openings. Create application packages in response to the opportunities you uncover.

- **Day 4:** Review the applications you've submitted recently; follow up through e-mail or phone calls to significantly boost your likelihood of landing an interview. Send out at least one "Consider me!" package.

- **Day 5:** Connect with at least one more person and inform them about your job search goals. Use e-mail, a phone call, an in-person meeting, or a group event to make this connection.

- **Day 6:** Devote another hour to reviewing your target company Web sites, as well as job sites, and responding to new opportunities.

Feel free to use these suggested plans as a framework for developing your own effective job search strategy, keeping in mind that you should devote about one-third of your time to each of the most effective job search avenues: responding to ads, approaching companies directly, and connecting with others.

Allow Yourself Enough Time to Establish a Successful Routine

As you begin implementing your job search plan and activities, it's very likely that things will feel awkward for a while. Studies show that a new routine takes nearly three weeks to become a habit for you, so don't worry if for the first several days, you feel as if you're living someone else's life. Just keep going through the motions and tweaking your activities until you find a routine that's comfortable for you.

Why It's Worth Doing

You've probably come across this definition for stupidity at some time in your life: Doing the same thing over and over, expecting a different result. If you've been frustrated with your job search results in the past, and you want to be more effective in the future, you'll *need* to try things differently. The job search activities described throughout this book have given you the knowledge for how to search more successfully. Now you need to implement those activities. Having a plan, complete with specific activities, a set routine, and an estimated timeline for completion, gives you the structure you need to achieve the results you want.

Career Champ Profile: Aileen

For months, Aileen had been pretty casual about her job search activities: She'd look at one or two job search sites every other day or so, and send out a resume occasionally. But she was getting increasingly frustrated with how long her search was taking. On average, she'd get a call for an interview about every other month.

"I'm ready to get more serious about this," she said. "I've figured out that I can get up a little earlier each day and spend an hour each morning devoted to job search activities." In line with her schedule, I talked her through a potential six-hour-per-week job search plan. She liked the idea of putting more effort into researching and contacting companies directly, as well as connecting with individuals more frequently. She left my office with a plan and to-do list in hand.

We talked a week later to see how things were going. "Weeeellll, I'll admit, getting into some of these new activities is harder than I expected it would be. For instance, I'd rather stay in bed than get up early!" We both laughed at that comment. "But I know that I need to be putting more time into this, so I've been getting up on schedule. Yet I'm struggling with other things, too. There's so much information about different companies out there, I don't know when to say, 'Enough!' And I'm a little nervous about contacting some of the people I know to meet with them about my job search. Overall, I feel pretty confused."

I encouraged Aileen to stick with the activities on her six-hour-per-week job search plan. "Your plan suggests that you spend about an hour researching target company information. So when that time is up, move on to another activity." She liked that idea. "And about connecting with people, remember, you can e-mail them with your request, or phone them when they're not likely to pick up. Plus it really helps to use the scripts we talked about—it takes the guess-work out of what to say. So give yourself a challenge to set up a meeting, and reward yourself when you have it scheduled."

When I talked with Aileen two weeks later, she was feeling much better. "This week, things started to 'click.' I feel like I have a rou-tine, and best of all, I feel like I'm *really* making progress on my job search. I have a meeting with a great contact tomorrow, plus I got called in for an interview next week. Things are starting to happen!"

Core Courage Concept

Devoting time to the things in life that are of the highest priority for you is one of the best gifts you can give yourself. Yet even if some-thing makes sense logically, emotionally it might be difficult for you to execute. So be kind and patient with yourself. Choose a job search plan that is truly workable for you, and aim to build momentum over time. Before you know it, you'll be humming along, and results will really begin to happen.

Confidence Checklist

☐ Calculate about how long your job search should take.

☐ Set up a job search plan that works for you.

☐ Allow yourself enough time to establish a successful routine.

Chapter 15

Troubleshoot Your Search and Improve Your Results

F rustrated with how your job search is going? Looking for some fast, effective fixes to improve your results? The information in this chapter will help you pinpoint potential problems and then provide you with specific strategies for blasting through roadblocks to keep moving forward.

Risk It or Run From It?

- **Risk Rating:** Some of the suggestions for solving job search challenges might feel a little outside of your comfort zone, but rest assured, detailed how-to info is provided in this book to show you exactly what to do to succeed.

- **Payoff Potential:** If you're sick and tired of getting nowhere in your search, and are ready to try new things for better results, the payoffs for you will be huge!

- **Time to Complete:** A minute or more, depending on the activities you choose.

- **Bailout Strategy:** For workarounds, check out the other suggestions provided in the chapters noted.

(continued)

(continued)

- **The "20 Percent Extra" Edge:** This short assessment and recommended list of improvements can help you find and fix job search problems quickly, helping you break out of the job search failure pattern.

- **"Go For It!" Bonus Activity:** Create a list of job search strategies that you need to improve; then create a plan, including deadlines, for accomplishing the items on your list.

How to Overcome Challenges and Succeed with Your Search

Wondering why things aren't going better for you in your search? It could be that by tweaking just one or two strategies, you could greatly improve your results. The two steps outlined in this chapter—diagnosing and then remedying any roadblocks that are holding you back—will allow you to quickly and successfully make better progress in your search.

Diagnose Your Job Search Difficulty

Take this quick quiz to determine potential problem areas that might be getting in the way of making better progress. Label the following statements "True" or "False":

Effective Job Search Activity	True	False
1. I have clearly defined the type(s) of job positions that I am aiming for.		
2. I have identified two or more industries that are a good fit for my specialty.		
3. I have researched 20+ companies within my target industries that could be potential employers for me.		

Effective Job Search Activity	**True**	**False**
4. I have an effective system for organizing data about companies and contacts, so that I can easily record my activities and locate information when necessary.		
5. I regularly review job posting sources (such as company Web pages, newspapers, and online job sites) to uncover new openings.		
6. When I respond to a job ad, I tailor my resume and cover letter to match the priorities of the position.		
7. I follow up after I have applied to openings to make sure my materials were received and to discover what will happen next.		
8. On average, I get called to interview for at least 10 percent of the positions to which I apply.		
9. When I uncover a job ad at a company that is a good fit for me, I research other similar businesses and send them information about me, also.		
10. I send a resume and letter of introduction to companies on my target list of employers—even if they have no open positions advertised.		
11. I have a list of people within my circle that could be supporters for me and I regularly connect with them about my job search.		
12. I have identified, and participate in, a few groups that are a fit for my personal and professional interests.		

(continued)

(continued)

Effective Job Search Activity	True	False
13. I am careful not to spend the majority of my time searching for and responding to online job ads. Rather, my job search activities are fairly equally balanced among applying to advertised openings, contacting potential employers directly (even if no job openings exist), and connecting with others to expand my circle of supporters.		
14. I feel good about the amount of time I am devoting to my job search based on what I am able to reasonably fit into my schedule.		

Panic Point! Did you answer "no" to most of these statements, and are you feeling like a job search failure? Don't! Keep in mind that *90 percent of job searchers don't make use of effective job search strategies,* so you're in the majority! Yet *you* have an edge on those searchers: You're actively seeking out ways to improve your results…and the strategies in this book will show you how to succeed. So erase your feelings of failure, and instead tell yourself, "I'm learning how to be a more effective job searcher!"

Remedy Job Search Weaknesses with Effective Strategies

For all of the statements in the quiz to which you responded with "True," check out these strategies for troubleshooting problem areas and getting your search on a more successful track:

1. "I have clearly defined the type(s) of job positions that I am aiming for."

Having a defined focus for your job search allows you to find work faster and easier, because you can more successfully identify potential employers, know where to look for opportunities, develop effective resumes and cover letters, and communicate your goals to others so that they can better help you. Strategies for more clearly defining your job search focus are described in chapter 3.

2. "I have identified two or more industries that are a good fit for my specialty."

Although you might be able to execute your work in a wide range of industries, trying to connect with hundreds of businesses across multiple segments is too "shotgun" to be effective. By selecting a few industries—2 to 10, for instance—you can more successfully research and link up with businesses and people within those industries, and achieve better, faster job search results. For suggestions on identifying industries that are a good match for your job search goals, check out chapter 4.

3. "I have researched 20+ companies within my target industries that could be potential employers for me."

A list of potential employers who are a good match for your career goals is one of your most valuable job search tools. With it, you have a clear idea of who should be aware of your background and expertise. Plus, by sharing it with your circle of supporters, they can more effectively connect you with companies and people that can help you move forward. For ideas on how to create your own valuable potential employers list, review the suggestions in chapter 4.

4. "I have an effective system for organizing data about companies and contacts, so that I can easily record my activities and locate information when necessary."

Keeping track of all of the details connected to the positions, companies, people, and activities involved in your job search can be an overwhelming task. Having an effective organization system can make the difference between managing your job search data successfully and getting frustrated and giving up altogether. An effective, easy-to-administer job search organization system is described in chapter 10.

5. "I regularly review job posting sources (such as company Web pages, newspapers, and online job sites) to uncover new openings."

Regularly reviewing posted job ads, using the resources that are the best match for your career goals, allows you to capitalize on fresh opportunities as soon as they become open. Be sure that at least once each week, you visit the Web pages for the companies on your target list, as well as check out postings in area newspapers, and on job Web sites that are a good match for your specialty.

6. "When I respond to a job ad, I tailor my resume and cover letter to match the priorities of the position."

It can take just a few minutes to customize your resume and cover letter to improve your chances for being called in for an interview. Simple steps, such as adjusting your career objective, adding in keywords, and highlighting certain aspects of your background, can significantly improve your results. Detailed how-tos for these strategies are described in chapters 5, 6, and 7.

7. "I follow up after I have applied to openings to make sure my materials were received and to discover what will happen next."

Although it can feel like a pretty scary step to take, a quick phone call to follow up on an application you've submitted can greatly improve your chances for being selected for an interview. To make this step more doable, call before or after regular business hours, and read a script like the ones included in chapter 8.

8. "On average, I get called to interview for at least 10 percent of the positions to which I apply."

A good guideline for gauging the effectiveness of your job application materials is to expect at least one interview for every 10 applications you submit. If you're not landing an interview 10 percent of the time (or more), your resume might benefit from improvements (see chapter 5, or check out *The Career Coward's Guide to Resumes* for recommendations), or your job search focus might require some tweaking (see chapter 3 for suggestions).

9. "When I uncover a job ad at a company that is a good fit for me, I research other similar businesses and send them information about me, also."

Since you've already put in the time and effort to customize your resume and cover letter for a specific job opening, one fast, effective strategy for improving your job search results is to research and send the same resume, along with a personalized letter of introduction, to other companies in the same industry. Chapter 8 provides details about this strategy.

10. "I send resumes and letters of introduction to companies on my target list of employers—even if they have no open positions advertised."

Since the majority of job openings are never advertised, and at least one-third of job opportunities get snatched up by job searchers who approach companies even if no job ad is posted, it only makes sense for you to make use of this avenue as well. If you haven't yet taken advantage of this effective method, see chapter 9 for how-to information.

11. "I have a list of people within my circle that could be supporters for me and I regularly connect with them about my job search."

People who know you and the quality of your work, and who are personally invested in seeing you succeed, can act as eyes and ears for you, on the lookout for good-fit opportunities. But they can only do so if they understand your job search goals. So take the time to connect with them and educate them about your job search focus. Several suggestions for linking up with your supporters are covered in chapters 12 and 13.

12. "I have identified, and participate in, a few groups that are a fit for my personal and professional interests."

    Hobby clubs, volunteer organizations, professional associations, and job search groups are all potential resources for expanding your circle of contacts so that others can help you in your hunt for a good-fit position. Each group has its own personality and purpose, so take the time to find a few that are a good fit for you. Ideas for locating and investigating potential groups are described in chapter 12.

13. "I am careful not to spend the majority of my time searching for and responding to online job ads. Rather, my job search activities are fairly equally balanced among applying to advertised openings, contacting potential employers directly (even if no job openings exist), and connecting with others to expand my circle of supporters."

    It's *so* easy to fall into the rut of spending hour after hour surfing the Internet looking for job ads. Yet studies show that this is one of the *least* effective methods for locating attractive job openings. To improve the success of your search, limit the time you devote to finding and replying to online ads to one-third or less of your activities.

14. "I feel good about the amount of time I am devoting to my job search based on what I am able to reasonably fit into my schedule."

    With everything else you have to juggle in your life, it's easy for your job search to get pushed down on your list of to-do's.

Developing an effective plan, and combining it with a schedule that allows you to make your job search a priority, enables you to meet your job search goals faster and easier. Even if you're able to devote only a few hours each week, you can continue to make steady progress. For ideas on how to make this happen for you, model job search plans and schedules are provided in chapter 14.

Why It's Worth Doing

Sometimes just a small change in what you're doing can change your results completely. Yet in the world of job searching, there are so many variables, it's difficult to know what to change! Working through the quiz in this chapter, item by item, helps you break down your job search into bite-sized pieces, and to evaluate each piece to determine how it's working (or not) for you. Then, once you have an idea of specific areas you can target for improvements, voilà, you have a step-by-step to-do list to achieve better results!

Career Champ Profile: Jorge

Jorge had so much to offer the right employer: He was highly skilled as a trainer on computer software applications, dedicated to delivering quality work, and excellent dealing with customers. If only he could find a position that would allow him to do to the work he loved to do!

He'd already been job searching for two months, and was getting frustrated with his minimal results. I walked him through the most common job search pitfalls, asking him about his current activities and results. When we hit on the activity of identifying other similar employers every time he applied to a posted job ad, and sending them a resume and letter of introduction, he sat up straighter and looked at me excitedly. "That's a great idea!" he said. "I hadn't thought of doing that, but it makes sense. I've already done the work of customizing my job search materials, so why not just send them out to a few more similar companies, right?"

Two weeks later Jorge sent me this e-mail: "Hi Katy, Just wanted to let you know that sending my resume to companies similar to places where I'd applied to an advertised job worked. One company contacted me two days after I'd sent my materials, and said that one of their training specialists had just given notice, and could I come in for an interview. I met with them two days ago, and they just called to offer me a job! Thanks for your idea!—Jorge" By changing his strategy just slightly, Jorge was able to accomplish his job search goals.

Core Courage Concept

None of us likes to find out we've been putting our time and effort into activities that aren't working well. In a way, it can seem easier to pull the covers over our heads and *just not know* what we're doing wrong. But ultimately, we want to connect with positions and people who will appreciate our expertise and help us move forward professionally. So even though it might feel a little touchy to analyze the weak points in your search strategy, keep the bigger goal in mind and be open to small changes that can lead to better results.

Confidence Checklist

☐ Remedy job search weaknesses with effective strategies.

☐ Diagnose your job search difficulty.

Chapter 16

Respond Effectively to Opportunities

Now all of the hard work you've put into your job search is beginning to pay off: You're getting referred to new contacts who can help you in your search; you're getting calls for interviews from the companies who have received your resume; plus you're seeing more and more opportunities to contribute as a valuable member of a company's team.

All of these possibilities are exciting—but you might also be feeling a little overwhelmed. How do you juggle all of these opportunities? What should you respond to first, second, and so on? In this chapter, you'll learn how to prioritize and effectively take action with the many doors that are opening for you.

Risk It or Run From It?

- **Risk Rating:** There's mid-level risk with these activities. You'll need to choose and prioritize your activities, and that can make Career Cowards squirm. But I'll equip you with effective decision-making tools so that you feel confident in deciding which steps to take, and in what order.

(continued)

(continued)

- **Payoff Potential:** Excellent! Making solid choices regarding how you spend your time will lead to better results.

- **Time to Complete:** Most of the strategies in this chapter will take you just a minute or two to complete.

- **Bailout Strategy:** Well, you can "wing it," handling opportunities as they come your way. But if you find that you have a landslide of possibilities to sort through, and are feeling snowed under, the strategies in this chapter can help you dig out successfully.

- **The "20 Percent Extra" Edge:** Knowing what to focus on first, and why, allows you to save time and increase your results.

- **"Go For It!" Bonus Activity:** Keep a running list of "to-do's" in a word-processing or spreadsheet file, reordering items based on their priority and urgency.

How to Successfully Handle the Many Possibilities Coming Your Way

Visualize this: You wake up Tuesday morning and check your e-mail. Your in-box shows two messages from HR reps at companies where you've applied, requesting interviews with you. There's also another message from a hiring manager at a local company you approached directly a few weeks ago, and he wants to meet with you, too. Plus your friend Richard, whom you met for coffee last week, has sent you an e-mail with the names of three people he suggests that you connect with, as they might be able to help you in your job search.

But that's not all: You're still thinking about the meeting you had with a company owner yesterday. She didn't have a job open, but it was obvious that you'd be a great fit for her company. You want to follow up with her to see if you can make something happen there. Oh, and there are also two e-mails about job openings that are a match for your background. You need to apply to those sometime. Finally, you don't want to forget about researching and sending your materials to those two new businesses you found out about yesterday. Wow, this is exciting, but a little overwhelming, too! How do you decide which of these opportunities you should respond to first, next, and so on?

Prioritize Your Opportunities

When an avalanche of opportunities and to-do's hits you all at once, it helps to have a plan for how to respond effectively. This step-by-step process will help you prioritize your opportunities and execute a successful response strategy:

1. **Remind yourself of your job search goals.** In chapter 3, you defined your job search focus. Look over what you defined at that time, as a reminder of what you're aiming for.

2. **Create a list of all of the opportunities and activities currently on your plate.** Putting everything on paper allows you to get the whirlwind of items out of your head, so that you can see how to deal with the possibilities more objectively. For instance, from the scenario described, you could create this list:

   - Follow up on the first message from the HR representative who wants to schedule a job interview with you.

   - Follow up on the second message from the HR representative who wants to schedule a job interview with you.

   - Contact the hiring manager at the company you approached directly to schedule a meeting.

   - Follow up with the first person Richard suggested that you contact.

   - Follow up with the second person Richard suggested that you contact.

   - Follow up with the third person Richard suggested that you contact.

- Draft a position proposal for the company owner you met with yesterday.

- Apply to the first job announcement you just received.

- Apply to the second job announcement you just received.

- Research and send direct-approach materials to the first new business you learned about yesterday.

- Research and send direct approach materials to the second new business you learned about yesterday.

3. **Determine the significance of each item on your list.** Each opportunity has a different level of "value" to you, depending on its potential to help you achieve your job search goals. Evaluating opportunities based on two criteria, importance and urgency, helps you decide how to prioritize your activities. For instance, you can rank the importance of an opportunity based on how closely it matches your job search goals, using an A, B, and C rating. Then in terms of urgency, you can use a 1, 2, 3 ranking system, with 1 being extremely urgent, 2 being less urgent, and so on. Using this ranking system, you might rate the items on your list in this way:

- Follow up on the first message from the HR representative who wants to schedule a job interview with you. **B1** (Why a B1? You need to reply promptly to be professional, but the job doesn't interest you that much.)

- Follow up on the second message from the HR representative who wants to schedule a job interview with you. **A1** (This job is very appealing to you, plus you want to get back to the HR rep quickly.)

- Contact hiring manager at the company you approached directly to schedule a meeting. **A1** (This company looks like a good match for you, plus you want to be professional and respond quickly.)

- Follow up with the first person Richard suggested that you contact. **B2** (You want to follow up with this person soon, but it doesn't need to be immediately.)

- Follow up with the second person Richard suggested that you contact. **B2** (Ditto above.)

- Follow up with the third person Richard suggested that you contact. **B2** (Ditto above.)

- Draft a position proposal for the company owner you met with yesterday. **A2** (This opportunity is highly important because you perceive a good match. But she's not expecting anything right away.)

- Apply to the first job announcement you just received. **B3** (The job seems like a so-so fit, plus the closing date isn't until next week.)

- Apply to the second job announcement you just received. **A3** (The job seems like a good fit, but the closing date isn't until two weeks from today.)

- Research and send direct-approach materials to the first new business you learned about yesterday. **C3** (You don't know much about this company yet, and they're not expecting anything from you, so there's no huge hurry.)

- Research and send direct-approach materials to the second new business you learned about yesterday. **C3** (Ditto above.)

4. **Create and implement your plan based on your ratings.** Now that you've ranked each activity, it's easy to prioritize your activities, putting the "A" and "1" items at the top of your list. For instance, the list from our example would look like this:

- Follow up on the second message from the HR representative who wants to schedule a job interview with you. **A1**

- Contact the hiring manager at the company you approached directly to schedule a meeting. **A1**

- Follow up on the first message from the HR representative who wants to schedule a job interview with you. **B1**

- Draft a position proposal for the company owner you met with yesterday. **A2**

- Apply to the second job announcement you just received. **A3**

- Follow up with the first person Richard suggested that you contact. **B2**

- Follow up with the second person Richard suggested that you contact. **B2**

- Follow up with the third person Richard suggested that you contact. **B2**

- Apply to the first job announcement you just received. **B3**

- Research and send direct-approach materials to the first new business you learned about yesterday. **C3**

- Research and send direct-approach materials to the second new business you learned about yesterday. **C3**

Once you have your action list prioritized, you'll have a clear plan for where to invest your time first, second, and so on. Using this system can significantly improve your efficiency and effectiveness in your job search.

Prepare Position Proposals for Great-Fit Possibilities

As you connect with and learn about businesses, there's a good chance that you might uncover opportunities where you could be a valuable addition to a company's team, but no job opening exists. When this happens, instead of letting a golden opportunity pass you by, you'll want to present the decision maker with a position proposal—a one-to-two page description of how you believe you could help the organization achieve its goals. Career Champ Carolina uncovered one of these opportunities. For suggestions on how to respond to an opportunity like hers, check out the "Career Champ Profile" section later in this chapter.

Why It's Worth Doing

Each day, we're presented with a multitude of opportunities, along with the power to choose what we will and won't act on. Unless we're careful about how we use our time, it's easy to let prime opportunities slip by simply because we didn't respond quickly enough.

Taking a few minutes each day to list and prioritize your activities and creating position proposals when you discover great-fit companies ensures that you invest your time and efforts into the opportunities that have the highest potential to yield the best results.

Career Champ Profile: Carolina

Talking with Carolina on the phone, it was obvious she was excited. "I had an incredible meeting with Rowan yesterday. She's the owner of a property management company I sent a direct-approach letter to a few weeks ago. She and her team are involved in exactly the kind of work I want to do, scoping out new properties, managing renovation projects, and working with the on-site management teams to reach maximum occupancy. Plus it sounds as if they're growing fast. Even though they don't have an opening now, I think I should make some kind of proposal to Rowan about how I could be an asset to their team."

I spent a few minutes talking with Carolina about how to put together a position proposal. "You want to communicate to Rowan that you have a good understanding of her needs, and how you can be an asset to her company. Be specific, but keep it concise—two pages or less. When you get a first draft done, e-mail it to me if you want me to look it over."

The next morning, I received an e-mail from Carolina with her position proposal attached. It emphasized how her background in property development and management could help Rowan's company achieve its business goals. "Now what do I do?" Carolina asked me in her e-mail. I wrote back that she should send a hardcopy, along with a brief cover letter, to Rowan. Also, I told her that she should request a short meeting to discuss her ideas. Carolina replied to my e-mail: "This makes me a little nervous, but I'm going for it anyway. Wish me luck!"

Two weeks later Carolina called me with an update. "My conversation with Rowan went really well. She loved my proposal and is going to look at her budget to see how soon she can add me to her team. This is a dream opportunity for me, and that position proposal was the key to making it happen!"

Figure 16.1 is a proposal similar to the one Carolina submitted.

**Position Proposal for Rowan Reiger,
Owner and President, Properties Plus!**

Dear Rowan,

After talking with you last week, I perceive a strong match between my skills and experience, and the future needs of your organization. Following is a brief summary of the areas where I believe I could make the greatest positive impact on Property Plus! Specifically, I could contribute to your organization in these ways:

Identifying and evaluating potential properties:

➢ My background includes 7 years of highly successful experience locating and assessing properties for development, acquisition, and renovation. The properties I have identified have consistently resulted in profitable increases to the bottom line.

Managing renovation projects:

➢ Over the last 10 years, I have managed more than 20 property renovation projects, with budgets of up to $2 million. I offer a proven track record for working successfully with architects, designers, and subcontractors to move projects forward successfully, and have completed every project assigned to me on time and within the established budget guidelines.

Working with the on-site management teams to reach maximum occupancy:

➢ In addition to identifying and analyzing opportunities, and working with teams to renovate properties, I have had extensive experience collaborating with on-site property management teams to attract and sign on leasing and rental clients to achieve maximum occupancy. My success rate in this area is attainment of 85 percent occupancy within 90 days of completion of renovation projects.

Rowan, I would welcome the opportunity to meet with you again to discuss the possibility of becoming a member of the Property Plus! team, either now or sometime in the future. In the next few days, I will follow up with you to confirm receipt of this proposal, and to determine a logical next step.

Thank you in advance for your consideration of my qualifications and interest.

Sincerely,

Carolina Posart

Figure 16.1: A proposal similar to Carolina's.

Core Courage Concept

When your hard work in job search begins to pay off, with many possibilities popping up all at once, it can seem exciting—but a little scary, too. It might seem easier to just "wing it," responding to things spontaneously, yet your lack of a plan might cause you to miss out on an important opportunity. Although prioritizing your activities might seem new to you, it's worth trying for a few days to see how it might benefit your job search progress. You might discover that you're able to accomplish more of what's truly important to you, in less time.

Confidence Checklist

☐ Prioritize your opportunities.

☐ Prepare position proposals for great-fit possibilities.

Chapter 17

Prepare and Perform Successfully in Interviews

ooray! Your hard work is resulting in job interviews. Invest just a little time in preparing for them and you can greatly increase your chances of receiving a job offer. In this chapter, I walk you step by step through a successful, get-ready-to-knock-'em-dead process.

Risk It or Run From It?

- **Risk Rating:** Pretty high. Not being prepared for an interview can quickly kill a good job opportunity.

- **Payoff Potential:** Pretty high, also. Being prepared for an interview often lands you that good job opportunity.

- **Time to Complete:** 30 minutes to a few hours, if you want to be thoroughly prepared.

- **Bailout Strategy:** You can rely on your wits, and hope your charm and good looks will be enough. But most candidates regret it when they don't prepare. At the very least, skim through this chapter to pick up some tips and then find ways to work in even just a little bit of preparation.

(continued)

(continued)

> - **The "20 Percent Extra" Edge:** Very few people adequately prepare for job interviews. By doing so, you successfully position yourself ahead of your competition.
>
> - **"Go For It!" Bonus Activity:** Create a video recording of a practice interview so that you can better see how you're presenting yourself.

How to Clinch Your Job Search Success Through Effective Interviewing

You know the saying, "20 percent of your effort yields 80 percent of the results"? This adage is particularly true when it comes to job interviews. To maximize your interviewing results, with a minimum amount of effort, follow the three proven steps outlined here:

- Identify the key tasks for the position.

- Brainstorm a few examples of your expertise in those areas.

- Practice your responses.

In just an hour or two, you can be well on your way to presenting your best self!

Pinpoint the Position's Most Important Responsibilities

The first step in preparing is to analyze the job description for the position and pull out the three to five most important requirements for the job. If you don't have a description, either guess your best about what the hiring company is looking for or call the hiring manager and ask for her list of priorities for the job.

Let's say, for instance, that you're scheduled to interview for a position as a veterinary technician at an animal hospital. The ad for the job reads like this:

Experienced, personable Veterinary Technician needed for busy animal hospital. Primary duties include greeting and providing basic support for patients and their owners, entering medical information into database and reporting programs, and cleaning cages and facilities to maintain a sanitary environment.

From this description, you can deduce that the following are the key responsibilities for this position:

1. Greeting and providing basic support for patients and their owners

2. Entering medical information into database and reporting programs

3. Cleaning cages and facilities to maintain a sanitary environment

Ideally, you'll want to choose the three to five responsibilities that are most important, even though there might be a number of other tasks in the job description. This will help focus your preparation activities in the most important areas. For additional suggestions on how to identify the most important responsibilities for a particular job, check out *The Career Coward's Guide to Interviewing.*

Develop Your Success Database of Examples

Once you've prioritized the position's responsibilities, you'll next want to brainstorm several examples of times when you've succeeded with those tasks in the past. For example, if you were interviewing for the vet tech position, you might ask yourself, "When have I greeted and provided basic support to animals and their owners?"

Panic Point! Typically, when I ask clients to brainstorm examples related to the key skills in a position, their immediate reaction is, "I can't think of any!" Usually, however, this is a panic response related to their fear that

(continued)

(continued)

> they won't have "the right stuff" to convince a hiring manager. Yet in my experience, once you take a deep breath and think about possible examples for a while, a number of them will come to you.

The following are some helpful resources for identifying possible examples:

- Resumes (both current and earlier versions)

- Performance reviews

- Letters of appreciation and congratulations from your supporters

- Any other resources that provide evidence of your experience and expertise, such as progress reports and school transcripts

As you read through these materials, ask yourself, "Did I use this particular skill here? As a part of this team? Working on this project?" Keep in mind that you don't need to identify examples that are *exactly* like what the job description asks for. A story demonstrating something similar is close enough. And chances are you'll be able to identify several instances (aim for at least three for each key skill area) that are possible success examples to be used in interviews. Once you've identified these examples, develop each of them into a "What, How, and Proof" story that will include the following details:

- **What:** *What* was going on? What happened to cause you to become involved in this activity? What problem needed to be solved, or what plan needed to be implemented?

- **How:** *How* did you handle the situation? How did you get the job done (the first step, next, and so on)? Provide a step-by-step account of your actions, even if it seems like way too much detail. You can edit out some of the finer points later.

- **Proof:** *Prove* that your efforts paid off. Did you do one or more of the following?
    - Save money
    - Make money
    - Improve quality
    - Improve the organization's image

  Name some results.

Focusing on the "When have I greeted and provided basic support to animals and their owners?" requirement, you might first come up with these examples:

- Supported patients with check-in procedures while working at a doctor's office.

- Worked as a dog walker.

- Took three classes on basic veterinary care through a local community college.

Then you can develop each one into a "What, How, and Proof" story, such as this:

- **What:** I once worked for Dr. Richardson, an ear, nose, and throat doctor who needed someone to provide front-desk support to patients as they arrived.

- **How:** I was responsible for greeting her patients when they arrived, verifying medical insurance information, having patients sign release forms, and entering patient data into the office's computer system.

- **Proof:** I know I was pretty good at this job because the patients frequently paid me compliments and told Dr. Richardson they thought I was polite and helpful. I was also given additional responsibilities—processing some of the medical insurance forms—only a few months after I had started there. Dr. Richardson said I was a quick learner and reliable.

This would be just one of the "What, How, and Proof" stories you would develop as part of your success database. Creating several of these stories (12 or more) will equip you with a toolbox of convincing, confidence-building examples to share in an interview. So then, when you're asked in an interview, "Have you ever worked in an office greeting patients before?" you can respond with, "Yes, I have. Would you like me to share an example?"

For more ideas on how to brainstorm and develop effective interview responses, check out the proven, powerful strategies described in the *Career Coward's Guide to Interviewing.*

Practice to Improve Your Performance

You've heard the saying, "Practice makes perfect." Well, I'm not a big believer in perfection (too much pressure!), but I do believe that practice can make a *huge* difference in how you perform in an interview, helping you present yourself more successfully and confidently.

An effective, confidence-building practice process includes these simple steps:

- Pull together or find a list of possible interview questions. This doesn't need to be a massive list of every potential question (you'll make yourself crazy!). Instead, start with the following list of 10 popular interview questions and add more if you choose:

    - Tell me about yourself.

    - What are your best strengths?

    - What weaknesses do you have that might hold you back in this job?

    - Give me some examples of times when you've held similar responsibilities as those required for this job.

    - What would your previous boss say about you?

- Why did you leave your last position? (Or, why are you leaving your current position?)

- What about this position appeals to you?

- What do you know about our company?

- What kind of money are you hoping to earn?

- Why should I hire you?

- Think through, and write down, some potential responses to these questions. Don't get too nervous about making your answers "perfect." View your notes as a first draft and just jot down some things to get started.

- Practice your responses out loud. Feel free to use your notes. Don't aim to memorize your answers (too stressful!). Rather, play with the content, reworking your answers, until you come up with responses that feel strong to you. If you're having trouble formulating your responses, ask a friend who is "good with words" for ideas. Sometimes it can be very helpful to get another person's input on how to phrase answers.

- Once you've worked out the basic content for your answers, practice, practice, practice saying them out loud until they begin to feel comfortable to you. Many candidates get especially nervous in interviews because they're trying to formulate and articulate their answers *for the first time* in the actual interview. This can be a formula for failure! By simply practicing your responses out loud, five times or more, you will significantly reduce your anxiety and improve your performance.

Why It's Worth Doing

Imagine trying to drive a car for the first time ever, along a busy highway, without ever being taught how or having had the chance to practice in a safe environment. Pretty scary, huh? I probably couldn't pay you to do it! Yet just like driving a car with no lessons, many job searchers take an, "I'll just stick my head in the sand and hope it works out okay" approach to preparing for interviews.

Just as finding out how a car works, learning what to do in certain driving situations, and practicing on a safe, empty road will greatly improve your results while driving in heavy traffic, thinking through some relevant examples, developing them into success stories, and practicing answers to popular job interview questions will significantly boost your success rate in interviews.

Career Champ Profile: Jesse

Jesse was an awesome software programmer. He could take on extremely challenging projects and quickly turn out awesome code. Yet he had a hard time communicating his strengths as a programmer in interviews. "I clam up, sweat, and can't think of anything good to say," he confessed to me.

After brainstorming some success stories that related to the jobs he'd been interviewing for, I asked him to take a list of popular questions, and to develop and practice responses to the items on the list. "The practicing part is *extremely* important," I emphasized. "Find some way to say your answers out loud at least five times each." I knew that Jesse did a lot of driving around town in his part-time job as a courier, so I made this suggestion: "Take the questions and answers along with you. When you stop at a light, practice an answer."

He reported on his progress at our meeting the next week. "The practice really made a big difference for me. After saying my answers out loud five times, they started to feel more comfortable. I've been modifying the content as I think of better, more concise ways to say what I want to say. I feel much less panicky already."

In his next interview, instead of drawing a blank (and sweating up a storm) when the hiring manager asked him questions, Jesse was composed and confident. It took him a few seconds to get rolling, and then the replies he'd practiced before the interview kicked in— and he received a job offer at his very next interview.

Core Courage Concept

Preparing for an interview, with all of the time, energy, and brain-power involved, can seem like an overwhelming project. Deciding to just "wing it" can seem easier—that is, until you get into the interview and realize you don't know what to say! Investing just an hour or two to brainstorm and practice success stories and interview responses (even if it seems scary at times) can mean the difference between "You're not what we're looking for" and "You're hired!"

Confidence Checklist

☐ Pinpoint the position's most important responsibilities.

☐ Develop your success database of examples.

☐ Practice to improve your performance.

Chapter 18

Prime the Pump for Future Career Successes

Whew! You've pushed yourself through the steps required to land a great position, and now it's paid off— you've accepted an offer for a job you love. Now it's time to take a well-deserved break from job searching, right? Well…you could take a break (at least a short one). But to truly keep your career moving forward, you'll want to build on the momentum you've already started, uncover better and better job opportunities, and achieve increasing levels of career success.

Risk It or Run From It?

- **Risk Rating:** Low to a little heart-pounding, depending on what you choose to do.

- **Payoff Potential:** Want to keep growing in your career? If so, it's definitely worth the effort!

- **Time to Complete:** A few hours each month.

- **Bailout Strategy:** You can put your job search and career maintenance activities on hold (most people do…), but at least skim through the ideas offered in this chapter, just in case you change your mind.

(continued)

(continued)

- **The "20 Percent Extra" Edge:** The majority of job searchers throw all of their momentum out the window after landing a job. By keeping just a little of your efforts moving forward, you effectively put yourself in the minority of fast-track career professionals.

- **"Go For It!" Bonus Activity:** Post your career vision in a place where you'll notice it often—it will help to keep you on the lookout for opportunities to realize your goals.

How to Attain Increasing Levels of Career Success

Think back over all that you've accomplished in your job search. Chances are that you've kicked off a chain of events that would result in even greater achievements if you kept moving forward on a few of these activities. Here you'll learn about a few simple, yet highly effective strategies to keep your career progressing—from maintaining the network of contacts and supporters you've developed, to targeting and connecting with the hiring managers who hold the keys to your next career opportunities. Investing just a little time and effort in these activities will pay back in big results!

Revise Your Career Vision

When you began this last job search, you had an idea about the kind of position you were hoping to land. This vision helped guide your decisions about what to highlight in your resume, which companies to add to your target list, and which success stories to share in job interviews. Now that you've taken the next step in your career, it's time to ask, "Where do I want to go from here?" For a while it might make sense to put your energy into mastering your new job. But a few months from now, it's likely that you will be evolving to have new career aims, as you learn about new opportunities and acquire new skills. So every six months or so, it makes sense to devote some time to considering additions and modifications to your career plan.

Here's a short career-visualization exercise from *The Career Coward's Guide to Changing Careers* to get you started.

To begin, find a quiet, pleasant place where you can think to yourself without interruptions for 30 minutes or so. It might be on a park bench, at a coffee shop, in your bedroom, or on a walk. Be sure to take along this book and note-taking materials. Once you're in your peaceful place, tell yourself to set aside the many thoughts and concerns that have been on your mind. You can go back to them again in a little while. But for now, your focus will be in visualizing your ideal career situation.

You are going to ask yourself questions and jot down your answers. If you're not able to think of an answer to a question right away, ask your mind to mull on it for a while, move on to another question, and then come back to the unanswered question later.

Picture yourself sometime in the future. It could be two years, or 10 or 20. Whatever timeframe works for you, so that you know you have had enough time to create the situation you are about to visualize.

Begin by writing down anything you see in your future picture. For instance, where are you? Are you indoors or outdoors? Is it a different city or country? What do you see around you? Describe the things you see. What's the weather like? What season is it?

Now ask yourself, what are you doing in this picture? What tools and materials are you working with? What do you spend your time talking or thinking about? Which activities give you joy and pleasure? What feels especially meaningful to you? How does your day progress? What new activities are you beginning?

In this picture, what topics, issues, or thoughts take your attention most of the time? What problems are you trying to solve, or what goals are you aiming to achieve? What benefits does your expertise create for others? What rewards do *you* receive from your work and activities? How are you compensated?

Other than yourself, who is in your picture? How do you interact with them? What purpose do they serve in your life?

Also, what other pieces of your life exist that are important to you but aren't in this picture that you're visualizing right now? What hobbies, places, activities, and events are you involved with at different times of the day, week, month, or year? Do you travel from one place to another? If so, where do you go? Who do you see and interact with during those times?

Looking even further into the future, what are your longer-term goals? What are your efforts leading toward? How are you progressing and developing yourself? What are you aiming to achieve ultimately?

Now, reflect on this life that you've created. What decisions have you made that support what is most important and meaningful to you? What values do you honor every day that help you to maintain your sense of respect for yourself and the world? What beliefs and standards do you live by?

Write down as many ideas as possible related to these questions. It might help to begin this exercise, leave it alone for a day or so, and then come back to it when your mind has been able to develop some further insights. When you've written down as many thoughts as you can (for now, at least), declare it "good enough!" and set it aside.

Now that you've created the beginning of a career and life vision, review it regularly to help keep you on track and moving forward, and make modifications once or twice a year to reflect your current goals.

Stay Connected with Your Supporters

Flip through the company/contact info pages you created throughout your job search to remind yourself of the many people you've met and connected with during your search. It's most likely an impressive list! Now that you've begun a professional relationship with people who can serve as valuable, long-term supporters for you (and you for them), maintain this important asset through one or more of the following strategies:

- Create a database of your contact information. In my many years as a career counselor, I can say that without question, the biggest regret of my career-minded clients is that they didn't track and keep up with the contacts they'd made over time. You can avoid this frustrating career gaffe by simply creating a file of your contacts' names, job titles, companies, and contact information (backed up regularly, of course!) in a database or spreadsheet program. You might also decide to store and update this important information using an online networking tool such as LinkedIn.

- Inform your contacts of your next career move. Now that you have your database, inform your supporters of your happy news. Have you accepted a promotion? Landed a new position at a different company? Launched your own business? Take the time now to e-mail or mail a brief announcement to the people who have been so helpful to you. Include your new business card and personally thank them for their support.

- Set up a schedule to stay in touch. Although it would be nice to get together every few months with every contact in your data-base of supporters, you might not have the time—especially if you're beginning a new position. So even if all you do is send a quick e-mail two times a year to say hello, update them on what's new with you, and ask how things are on their end, that quick check-in can be very effective for maintaining your pro-fessional relationship. Sending holiday cards—hardcopy or electronic—provides an ideal opportunity to say hello.

- Find ways to return the favors that have been granted to you. Whenever possible, provide support for the people who have so generously assisted you. If one of your contacts is job searching, offer to meet with him or her to brainstorm next steps. If a contact is building a customer list, do what you can to recommend and use the products and services offered. If you're asked to volunteer to support a community need, find a way to assist the effort.

Refresh Your Target Company List

You've invested a significant amount of time and effort into researching and building your target list of potential employers. Maintain and increase the value of this important asset by staying up on the changes happening in your specialty and industry. The following activities will help you maintain a current, valuable target list:

- **Become an active member of professional associations.** This activity will allow you to meet people in your industry and help you keep up on target company developments.

- **Follow the business news in the industry publications that pertain to your specialty.** This resource for news updates will keep you in-the-know on recent developments.

- **Research new companies and people as you find out about them.** And to keep your professional network growing and healthy, introduce yourself to new contacts to keep yourself competitive and known in your market.

Sharpen Your Skills Often

Yes, yes, I know...it's a pain to keep up on the latest technologies and processes affecting your career. But you *don't* want to be caught unprepared when a choice opportunity presents itself! To help you prioritize which skills you should develop, keep tabs on the technologies and processes being covered at national conferences within your specialty. Then propose to your employer that he or she invest in your training. In most cases, enhancing your skills will make you more productive on the job—and more competitive in the job market.

Act on Awesome Opportunities

Excellent opportunities for growing and achieving in our careers are all around us, every day. But to capitalize on them, we need to keep our eyes open to possibilities (some of them are well disguised!) and be ready to act on them when they appear. Maintaining your contacts, keeping your target list up-to-date, and regularly polishing your skills will help you uncover attractive career options. When you do identify an appealing opportunity, move things along by connecting with the decision makers who have the power to say "yes!" and by preparing and submitting proposals, like the one described in chapter 16. Don't let golden career opportunities pass you by.

Why It's Worth Doing

"Some people just seem to have all the luck." I've heard this statement from several individuals who were frustrated with their career situations. From their perspective, it seems that those people who are doing well in their careers are just getting fortuitous breaks, with very little effort at all. Yet in my conversations with people who are happy and growing in their careers, it's obvious to me that instead of having lucky breaks just land in their laps, they are constantly on the lookout for — and are responding to — opportunities that pop up on their radar screens. If they hear about a new business that could be a potential customer or employer, they research the organization and find ways to connect with company representatives. If they see a chance to apply their skills and experience in new, more rewarding ways, they put in the effort to move forward on their ideas.

Sure — acting on possibilities can seem scary, and you might wonder whether it's even worth the effort. Chances are that a good number of your attempts won't go anywhere. But if you're consistently identifying and acting on opportunities, a few are bound to go your way…and you'll experience steady career progress and successes.

Career Champ Profile: Gillian

A few years ago, Gillian made a career change from managing sporting-goods stores to recruiting engineers and technical professionals within the computer industry. Shortly after accepting her first position in her new career field, she sent an e-mail announcement to people she knew within the sporting-goods industry, as well as her former teachers and the contacts she'd made while researching and executing her career change. Altogether, she sent the following e-mail to about 50 people:

> Dear _____,
>
> I just wanted to let you know that I've accepted a new position as a technical recruiter with Talent Teams. I will be working with this organization to locate and place technical specialists with companies in the computer industry.
>
> Thank you for the support you have given me so far in my career. I am excited about this new opportunity, and I'll keep you posted on how things progress. In the meantime, please keep me in mind if I can support you in any way. My new contact information is listed below.
>
> Sincerely,
>
> Gillian Tiler
>
> Talent Teams
> gilliantiler@talentteams.com
> www.talentteams.com
> (970) 333-2222

After Gillian had settled into her new position, she began setting up coffee or lunch meetings with people in her network about once each week. She also kept her eyes open for articles and information that people in her network of contacts might like to read, and mailed those whenever she found something valuable. And at the start of each year, she sent cards wishing her contacts a successful and happy New Year.

About two years after beginning her new position with Talent Teams, Keaton, one of the contacts in Gillian's circle, called her to let her know that he'd just heard about an opening for a staff recruiter with one of the growing software companies in town. "Let me know if you're interested," Keaton told Gillian, "I know the owner and I can put in a good word for you." It turned out that Gillian was interested, and with Keaton's introduction, she was able to set up an interview and receive a job offer for 20 percent more pay than she was making at Talent Teams.

Core Courage Concept

No doubt about it...to keep redefining what you want out of your career by continually taking small steps toward achieving your goals takes guts, persistence, and a belief that your hard work will pay off. Yet Brian Tracy, my favorite motivational speaker, says it beautifully: "You are fully responsible for everything you are, everything you have, and everything you become." When it comes to your career, my wish is that you'll continue to challenge yourself (just an inch at a time!) to be your best. Go for it!

Confidence Checklist

☐ Revise your career vision.

☐ Stay connected with your supporters.

☐ Refresh your target company list.

☐ Sharpen your skills often.

☐ Act on awesome opportunities.

Index